The Well-Rounded Herbalist

Some books focus on growing herbs or cooking with herbs—others focus on herbal remedies or on their magical properties.

Until now, beginning gardeners had to search through many different books to dig up information on all aspects of a given herb's use and significance. *The Green Guide to Herb Gardening* has done all the groundwork on ten of the most popular, easy-to-grow herbs for you. Explore each herb's folklore and magic; growing, harvest, and storage preferences; medicinal properties; and culinary, cosmetic, and ornamental uses.

Once you reap your own aromatic harvest, you can use your herbs and *The Green Guide* to whip up mouth-watering lemon balm pesto, crowd-pleasing thyme fish filets, or any of over 90 other herb-enhanced beverages and foods.

Find out how easy and rewarding herb gardening can be, with the help of *The Green Guide to Herb Gardening*.

About the Author

Deborah C. Harding (Ohio) has studied herbs and gardening for many years. She and her husband, Tony, publish the Pryme Thyme Newsletter, an on-line almanac of gardening tips and seasonal recipes and traditions.

To Write to the Author

If you wish to contact the author or would like more information about this book, please write to the author in care of Llewellyn Worldwide and we will forward your request. Both the author and the publisher appreciate hearing from you and learning of your enjoyment of this book and how it has helped you. Llewellyn Worldwide cannot guarantee that every letter written to the author can be answered, but all will be forwarded. Please write to:

Deborah C. Harding
℅ Llewellyn Worldwide
P.O. Box 64383, Dept. K430-8
St. Paul, MN 55164-0383, U.S.A.

Please enclose a self-addressed, stamped envelope for reply, or $1.00 to cover costs. If outside U.S.A., enclose international postal reply coupon.

THE GREEN GUIDE TO HERB GARDENING

FEATURING THE 10 MOST POPULAR HERBS

DEBORAH C. HARDING

2000
Llewellyn Publications
St. Paul, Minnesota 55164, U.S.A.

First Edition
First Printing, 2000

Cover design: Lisa Novak
Interior art: Carrie Westfall
Cover photo: Ron Van Zee
Cover herb pot: Melon Patch Herbs
Editing and book design: Tom Lewis

Library of Congress Cataloging-in-Publication Data
Harding, Deborah C.
   The green guide to herb gardening: featuring the 10 most popular herbs / Deborah C.
       Harding.
       p. cm.
   Includes bibliographical references (p.).
   ISBN 1-56718-430-8
    1. Herb gardening. 2. Herbs. 3. Cookery (Herbs) I. Title.

SB351.H5 H28 2000
635'.7—dc21   99-049986

Llewellyn Publications
A Division of Llewellyn Worldwide, Ltd.
P.O. Box 64383, Dept. K430-8
St. Paul, MN 55164-0383, U.S.A.
www.llewellyn.com

 Printed in the United States of America on recycled paper

CONTENTS

DEDICATION

Special thank-yous to my proofreaders, Christa McNicholas and Linda Woolford. Another thanks to Audrey Abbott who read my manuscript and gave me some good ideas. Thanks to Yasmine Galenorn, fellow author, who led me to seek Llewellyn as my publisher and who helped me with the magical uses of herbs. Thank you to my parents, Vernon and Ida Mae Symes, who encouraged my writing "fetish" when I was young. A special thanks to my husband, Tony, for doing most of the housework so I could finish this project and to my daughters, Dana and Callie, for understanding that Mommy was really busy and couldn't spend as much time with them as they would have liked.

This book is dedicated to a woman who started me on my journey into the herbal world, Arlene Adkins. Remember, I wasn't the one who wanted to learn about herbs, it was my husband: now look what you've done! All my love.

INTRODUCTION

To many people, herbs are merely weeds to be plucked from the earth and thrown away, never to be seen again. To other people, herbs are magical, enchanting entities capable of changing the taste of food, to heal, make your skin and hair glow, or be woven into wreaths in which each plant used has a symbolic meaning.

Historically, herbs have been shrouded in folklore and mysticism. These magical plants have been associated with the ancient Druids who used them to heal and to see the future. They have been allied to witches whose concoctions gave them the ability to cast charms and spells. Individuals who understand the uses of herbs are sought after to share their knowledge. In a world of chemical preparations and preservatives these people comprehend the natural, old fashioned way, the way of the earth—a better way.

Herbs are a wonderful addition to any landscape. They can be incorporated into your flower or vegetable garden, or they can complete a garden theme.

Contrary to popular belief, most herbs are very easy to grow. In fact, they grow so well they are sometimes actually referred to as weeds. Herbs can even grow in drought conditions: they love bad soil and lots of sun. They need little care. What more could you ask for from a plant?

My husband wanted me to subtitle this book "How to Become the Neighborhood Witch." It seems everyone comes to our door to find alternative ways of treating everyday maladies such as scrapes and stings. They request recipes for herbal teas to induce sleep or herbal mixtures to place in their baths after a hard day's work for relaxation. Whenever they need a touch of thyme or parsley to put on their roast they know where to go.

When I began my journey into the world of herbs I was only interested in their culinary properties. Soon I began to see that the mint I used to make jelly for lamb could be used to make a tea to soothe the stomach after eating too much of the lamb. With just this one plant I could concoct an astringent for my face, I could disinfect an insect bite or create a Christmas potpourri.

There were so many uses for just one plant. To find all these wonderful methods of herbal use I had to search through multitudes of books. One book couldn't give me all the information I needed to start my new hobby. Some books explained how to cultivate, some how to cook with herbs, some gave remedies, and so on. I decided there was a real need for a reference book that would illustrate cultivation and usage for just a few simple herbs, from start to finish, including the basic properties of each.

In this book, I have taken ten of the herbs which are the easiest to grow and most useful, and will explain what they look like, their history, magical properties and folklore, propagation and how to grow them, their harvest and storage methods, and their uses (culinary, remedies, aromatic, cosmetic, ornamental, etc.). I would suggest that the novice herb gardener begin with five or six of the herbs described here, then add one or two the following year. Keep adding until you have all ten. This will give you a well-rounded herb garden.

The Green Guide to Herb Gardening should be all you will need to begin. As your knowledge grows, you can branch out to other, more technical publications, many of which I have outlined in bibliography at the end of the book. This is not intended to be a definitive book on herbs. There is so much knowledge about these magical plants no one book can contain it all. After seventeen years of herbal study I am still learning: it never ends.

Let me point out here that the remedies described in this book are based on traditional folk treatments. As such, they are not proven cures. If you have extreme symptoms, please consult a doctor immediately.

To use this book effectively, begin with the first chapter on propagation, preparation, and preservation. This is a must-read section. It will give you basics on how to get started with your herbs. If you come across a word you don't understand, refer to the glossary at the end of the book.

- The propagation section explains different methods for growing your herbs by seed, division, layering, stem cuttings, and root cuttings.
- The preparation section explains how to use you herbs in infusions or tea, tisanes, decoctions, tinctures, elixirs, and poultices.

- The preservation section discusses the methods of saving your herbs for future use by freezing and by air drying, oven drying, or using the microwave and dehydrator in drying. Preservation of herbs in oils and vinegars will be considered in detail.

Now, get ready to pick your herbs and get planting!

1
PROPAGATION, PREPARATION, AND PRESERVATION

Before you begin cultivating a passion for herbs, you should get to know the three aspects of herb gardening and use: propagation, or how to raise herbs from the ground up; preparation, or how to make mature herbs ready for use in foods or as a remedy; and preservation, or how to make the most of your herbs beyond the growing season. The following chapter covers the basics, before we move on to the individual herbs.

PROPAGATION

Propagation is the method by which new plants are created. There are several different ways to propagate a plant.

Seeds

Seeds should be planted in an enriched planting medium made of 1 part potting soil (from a garden center—not out of the ground), 2 parts vermiculite, and 1 part peat moss.

To make 12 cups of planting medium, combine 3 cups potting soil, 6 cups vermiculite, and 3 cups peat moss.

This medium is light and allows seeds to grow easily. Soil from the ground has many contaminates that will prevent your seeds from developing. It's also dense and makes it harder for your seedlings to emerge.

Some seeds need to be soaked in water to soften their outer shells, others need to be frozen or refrigerated for a time. Some need darkness to grow. Certain seeds need light. Some seeds are large and can easily be planted, while others are tiny and impossible to separate. Several seed varieties need bottom heat while others need no special care at all: just plant them outside and watch them grow. All of these possibilities are discussed in each individual chapter that follows.

Prepare your pots, flats, or whatever you might be using to start your plants. I prefer seed trays. They have tiny compartments, one per seed, with a watering tray beneath. Alternately, you can use whatever you have around the house. Used margarine containers or the bottoms of plastic pop bottles work quite well.

Germination

Seeds should be started 6 to 8 weeks before the last frost of the year. I live in the northeast of the United States and usually plant the first week in June. That means I begin germinating my seeds from the first through the third week in April, depending on the germination time for each seed. This gives the new plants enough time to grow and then get used to being outdoors before being planted. This process is called "hardening off"—a gradual exposure to weather and sun.

Place seeds in your containers, and for those that need darkness to germinate, cover with a thin layer of planting medium. For those requiring light, just press the seeds down into the planting medium without covering them. Place plastic or glass over the top of the containers. Keep moist by "bottom watering" (placing water in a tray below the container) or by removing the plastic or glass, misting gently with a spray bottle, then replacing the cover. The plastic or glass retains moisture and you won't need to water for several days.

Some seeds need bottom heat, which can be achieved in several ways:

Method 1—Place seed trays on top of the refrigerator.

Method 2—Purchase a commercial seed bottom warmer.

Method 3—Suspend metal shop lights from the ceiling with hooks and chains. Install fluorescent or grow lights. Bring the shop light down low and place your seed trays on top of the lights. Once your plants have sprouted you can take them off and pull the lights up so the seedlings are placed underneath the lights.

Method 4—Use waterbed heaters on a 70 to 75 degree setting (Note: all temperatures throughout this book are in Fahrenheit). Place a towel on top of the heater then place your trays or pots on top making sure the probe is under the towel topped by a tray or pot.

NEVER use a heating pad. These devices weren't made to be left on for long periods of time. Plus, if you get a heating pad wet, you're in big trouble.

As soon as the plants sprout, remove the covering plastic or glass. If your seeds are large, you probably only planted one seed per compartment or area in your pot, but if they were tiny it seedlings will need to be

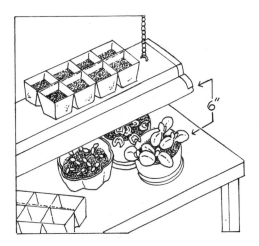

thinned. Pull out the weakest seedlings, leaving the strongest and healthiest one of the bunch.

Place your seedlings under grow lights or place them in indirect or filtered sun. Putting them in direct sun could cook them to death. Your seedlings will need at least twelve hours of light per day. Remember to turn your containers everyday if you are putting them in the sun: this will guarantee that your seedlings will grow straight.

The second set of leaves a plant grows are its true leaves. As soon as these leaves appear, they are ready to be potted in larger pots. Use margarine containers, poke holes in the bottom, using the lids as trays. The bottoms of plastic bottles can also be used for this purpose: just cut off the upper part of the bottle. You can usually plant 2 or 3 seedlings in each medium-sized container or bottle bottom. Use the same planting medium described earlier in this chapter.

Now that your plants have three or four rows of leaves and stand a few inches high (depending on the plant), they're ready to be hardened off. They must become accustomed to the weather, sunlight, or lack thereof. When the temperature becomes moderate (around 65 to 70 degrees), place your containers outside in a shady area for a few hours. Each day, leave them out a little longer, then begin to move them into the sunlight for a period of time. If the temperature falls below 60 degrees, make sure you bring them in or protect them in a garage or other shelter. Soon they will be ready to plant.

Layering

This is a very-time consuming but reliable method. Begin in the summer with low-growing herbs. Choose a branch near the base of the plant and strip it of the leaves near the branch's base. Touch this stripped area to the soil and press into the ground. Secure in place by pinning with a "U"-shaped wire. Keep the soil moist at first, then

regular watering will do. By the end of the growing season your new plant will be established. Cut the connection to the original plant and transplant.

Division

This method is better achieved in the early spring. You will need a shovel and a sharp knife. Herbs have underground roots, bulbs or tubers. Dig up a clump of herb with your shovel. With a knife cut or separate the clump into smaller sections about the size of your fist. Replant in the ground or in pots immediately.

Stem Cuttings

This method is best done in spring or late summer. Select mature stems about 3 to 4 inches long with no blooms. Strip leaves from the stem bottom, dip in water, then in rooting hormone. Set in a pot containing rooting medium (1 part peat moss to 3 parts vermiculite). Water well and cover with a plastic bag.

Again, I use margarine containers or pop bottles as containers. Make sure the plastic bag doesn't touch the plant by inserting popsicle sticks or pencils in the medium around the plant and propping the plastic bag on them. Place in indirect sun and keep watered by placing water in a tray underneath the plant; this will retain high humidity, which the plant needs at this stage. You can tell there's humidity if the plastic bag has drops of water on the inside. Remove the bag to mist if there is no moisture collecting, then re-bag. New growth is a sign that your new plant has developed roots. You can then remove the plastic bag, water normally, harden off, and plant.

Root Cuttings

Make root cuttings in the spring to plant in summer or in the fall to pot for Christmas presents. Carefully dig up a portion of an established plant and remove a root. Cut this root into 2-inch pieces. Fill a pot with a mixture of

1 part sand and 1 part peat moss. Place the root sections in pots, one per pot (time for those margarine containers and pop bottles again). Cover with 1 inch of the mixture. Moisten with a mist and place a plastic bag over top as in stem cuttings to reserve humidity. Place the pot in indirect sun and keep moist. When greenery sprouts, remove the plastic bag and water normally until the cutting is big enough to plant outside.

Check each chapter to find the best method of propagation for each herb. Now let's move on to preparations and methods for using your herbs.

PREPARATION

For a beginner, talk of infusions, tinctures, syrups, fermentations, and poultices can make their preparation seem tricky and very confusing. The following explanations will help you make these concoctions with ease.

Infusion

Think of tea when you think of infusions. Spring water is brought to a boil, removed from the heat and the herb is steeped (infused). You'll usually use 1 tablespoon of the fresh herb or 1 teaspoon of the dried to 1 cup of water for a regular infusion. Double the herb to make a strong infusion: leaves or flowers of the plant can be used. Cover and steep the infusion for 10 to 15 minutes (I usually steep by covering my cup with a saucer). This keeps the important oils in the infusion so they can be ingested instead of being lost as steam into the air. Infusions can be drunk hot or cold, and some are used externally. Check each herb chapter for uses.

Decoction

Decoctions are made from root, bark, or seeds, and sometimes from the stems of herbs. Combine 2 teaspoons dry or 2 tablespoons fresh herb to 2 cups of spring water. Bring this to a boil and simmer 10 to 20 minutes. Steep until cool, then strain. Use an enamel or glass pan, NEVER aluminum (aluminum will cause an unwanted chemical reaction with the liquid). The difference between an infusion and a decoction is the what part of the herb is used and when the water is boiled.

You can keep the difference between infusions and decoctions straight by simply remembering that infusions use leaves and flowers added after the water has been boiled, while decoctions use root, bark, seeds, and stems which are added to the water and then boiled.

Tisane

Tisanes (from Greek *ptisane*, meaning "crushed") were originally made from barley water. Barley was cooked in water and the water was then preserved in jars. While the water was still hot, herbs were infused in it. These days, hardly anyone uses this preparation.

If you want to try making one, set herbs and flowers in boiling spring water. Instead of steeping for 10 or 15 minutes, as you would for an infusion, you should only steep for about 5 minutes. Also, about twice as much of the herb should be used when making a tisane.

Tincture

Tinctures are made from an herb solution concentrate and alcohol. Water is usually added to this mixture as a way of diluting it. Tinctures are used in remedies and cosmetic applications. They can be stored for a long time because of their alcohol content, which is usually sixty percent or more. Vodka works best for this, since it has little or no taste. Herb roots, barks, or seeds are typically used in making tinctures.

To make a tincture, take 4 to 5 ounces of the herb and add 1 pint of alcohol. Soak anywhere from 2 to 6 weeks, shaking the jar daily. Once the tincture has taken on the scent of the herb, it will need to be strained through several layers of cheesecloth or coffee filters. Store in a dark bottle in a place away from light.

Elixir

Probably the most famous herbal preparation of all was the legendary "Elixir of Love." Elixirs are similar to tinctures. Infuse two rounded tablespoons of herb in 2 cups water for about 10 minutes. Add ½ cup of vodka. Strain. Add honey, which will act as a preservative.

Poultice

Remember those old mustard plasters? They were a form of poultice. A poultice consists of bruised fresh hot herbs. The plant matter is applied to the affected area and a hot cloth is wrapped over them.

PRESERVATION

There are several different methods to preserve the herbs you grow. Freezing and drying are both the most common options.

Freezing

This is an effective way to preserve herbs if you have the room in your freezer. Some herbs need to be plunged into boiling water, ice water, or both before freezing, while others must be stripped from their stems. All should be cleaned before being preserved.

Freezer bags are the best when storing herbs preserved by freezing. Most herbs can be stored in a freezer for one year and still retain their potency. The herb will retain its color in most cases, but when it is defrosted it will become limp and sometimes a bit slimy. For this reason, frozen herbs are best used in soups or stews.

Drying

Dried herbs can be stored in airtight bags or jars. Plastic containers are not recommended, since plastic tends to take on the smell of what comes in contact with it. You may be dooming a particular container to hold only a certain herb for the rest of its days. Herbs kept in clear jars must be stored in dark areas, so that their color won't fade from exposure to light. For that reason, colored jars are better for herb storage, brown or dark blue being the best: I use iced tea jars. Just make sure you label your jars or you're likely to be using basil instead of mint for some things. If your labels fall off, follow the "nose knows" rule: open the lid and sniff out what herb you have.

Herbs can be dried in several ways.

Air Dry—For air-drying, tie several branches of a washed and towel-dried herb in bundles with rubber bands. Hang these bundles upside-down in a well ventilated area: an open barn or garage is a good place, even an attic will work. Each herb takes a different amount of time to dry. When the herb crackles when touched, it is ready to be stripped from the stem and placed in containers. You can also strip fresh herbs from their stems, place them in an open-weave basket, and suspend the whole thing from the ceiling. Another method is to lay the leaves on a screen until dry. Some herbs may lose their color and turn dark using this method, but their essential qualities will be preserved.

Oven Dry—In this method you need to strip the fresh herb from its stem and place the pieces on a cooking sheet in a thin layer, preventing each leaf from touching the others. Place in an oven with a pilot light until dry. You may have to stir the herb around occasionally. It may take a few days for the herb to dry completely. If your oven doesn't have a pilot light, set it at the lowest temperature, keeping the door open a little at the top and stirring your herb every now and then. This will take several hours. Best results can be had with gas ovens. Sometimes an herb gets burned if it's being dried in an electric oven, resulting in a burnt taste.

Microwave—In my opinion, the microwave method is the best. Most herbs retain their flavor and color with this method, and it's fast and easy, too. Clean the herb and strip leaves from the stems. Place the leaves between two paper towels. Make sure the leaves don't touch each other. Microwave on high for 1 minute. Check for crispness and continue to microwave at 30-second intervals checking the herb each time. Remember that the herb will continue to "cook" for a few seconds after the micro-wave turns off. When the herb feels warm but leathery it is probably done. Set aside for

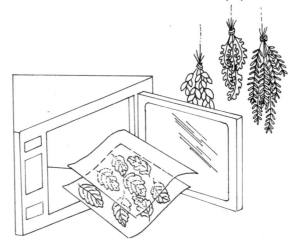

a few minutes and check again when it cools to see if it is totally dry. If not, repeat the above steps.

Dehydrator—The Dehydrator Method works great, but only if you have a screen for your dehydrator. Herbs have a tendency to break apart and fall through the cracks in your dehydrator if you don't have a screen.

Certain herbs can be stored in vinegar or oil, then stored in the refrigerator. These will last anywhere from 3 to 6 months. Check individual chapters for instructions, and consult the glossary at the end of the book for a handy guide to the terms used here.

This chapter has revealed how to grow and preserve your herbs. But you could cultivate herbs your whole life and never experience a deeper, more magical aspect of the world of herbs. So, in the next chapter, we'll look at the ways herbs can be used for magic and healing.

2

A WORD ON THE
MAGIC USES
OF HERBS

Herbs are truly magical. This magic lies in an herb's use, whether it is bringing sleep to the insomniac, making your hair shine with highlights, conditioning your skin, relaxing tired and sore muscles, steeping a delightful tea, or acting as a component in a protection charm. Many herbs are employed by magic users to cast spells, create potions, and make amulets.

Before going any further, I should point out that I am not a magic user myself: the magical uses of the herbs appearing in each chapter are basic to the properties of those herbs. They deal with folklore and superstition, rather than actual magic. This means you won't find recipes for potions or instructions for spells in the following pages, since I am not knowledgeable in those subjects. What you will find is a historic representation of how each herb has traditionally been used for protection, guidance, or to gain wealth and love.

As I conducted my research in magical herbs, I was amazed at how many things my family and friends do which are considered magical. I thought these things were second nature or, at least, superstitions not to be trifled with. For instance, a friend told me to carry a piece of basil with me when I traveled so that I would come home safe. And I've always known that it is bad luck to give parsley away.

Magic is nothing to play with. Trying to perform spells without having knowledge is a very dangerous thing to do. While calling on the powers that help achieve magic, one can open the door to forces that can overpower and manipulate even the strongest individual. I urge you to leave the potions, spells, and other magical tools to those who understand them and can use them wisely and safely. If you do plan to learn about magic, please seek out a practitioner who can teach you in person. There are some very good books on the market concerning magic and herbs. The most informative concerning actual magical acts are by Scott Cunningham. Another good source for spells, visualizations, tools, and other equipment for magic and herbs is Yasmine Galenorn's book *Embracing the Moon* (Llewellyn Publications, 1998). Both these sources will give you a good background on the use of magic.

There are several ways to prepare your herbs in a safe manner for use as protective charms, as blessings, as guides for success and prosperity, and to purify your surroundings. Remember that your herbs should never, in any manner, do harm or be made to manipulate anyone. They are only to be used to enhance goodness and light.

Most practitioners suggest the importance of preparing your body and mind before beginning to use your herbs in any magical sense. Cast out any negative thoughts and become as tranquil as possible. You should prepare your surroundings so that you won't be disturbed. Also, your area should be clean and comfortable. Everything you need to make your charm should be nearby and all the necessary tools should be clean as well. In many cases, your herbs will have to be ground before using them: while grinding, keep in mind the intent for which the herb will be used. For example, if you are grinding basil for a charm that will protect a

home, keep in mind this intention, its recipients, and the blessings that will come from within to fill the home. If any negative thoughts filter through, fling them away or stop immediately until you can overcome them.

One way you can prepare your herbs to be used for magical purposes is to make a sachet. Used to scent drawers or closets, they are little "pillows" of cloth, tied up and decorated, containing herbs. Make a magical sachet by placing the desired herb in the middle of a white cloth, about four inches square. Bring all the corners of the cloth together and tie with a red ribbon. The color white symbolizes the purity of the intent. You are not making this sachet with the purpose of doing harm. The color red symbolizes the passion that gives you the desire to make the sachet and do good. Other colors can be used to match the sachet's intended use. Use a white cloth and colored ribbon or a colored cloth and white ribbon.

You will notice many strands of historical tradition throughout this book. One of the most influential traditions was what is known as the "Victorian Language of Flowers." This was a practice in nineteenth-century England to give different flowers "secret" meanings. Both fresh flowers and dried bouquets were given to indicate a particular feeling. One example of this is when rosemary was incorporated into a bouquet of red roses: the meaning of this was love and remembrance, and it was a gift usually given to women by their men as they went off to war. While not directly magical, the power of symbolism reflects in the use of flowers, how they are incorporated in remedies, and the intentions associated with them.

Color is also as important as the kind of flower or herb in this symbolism. The following is a color chart that will give you the intent for the colors utilized.

Color	Intent
Dark Blue	Joy
Light Blue	Inspiration, peace, tranquillity
Brown	Money, business
Gold	Success, good luck
Green	Prosperity, fertility
Orange	Healing
Pink	Love, friendship
Red	Passion, love, courage
White	Purification, healing, purity
Yellow	Healing

Different people use colors in many different ways. Not every practitioner will use orange for healing. They may use red or another color. The correspondences shown on this chart are recommendations based on standard uses.

Another way to use herbs magically is through herbal oil. Essential oils can be purchased in many pharmacies and specialty stores. It takes too much of the herb for anyone to make a practical quantity of oil themselves, so it's better to find some produced commercially. Oils can be used to scent the room or the body. If you are placing oil on the skin, you must first test to make sure you aren't allergic to the oil. Place a small amount on your wrist or inner arm. The skin will redden and itch if you are allergic to it. See each chapter to learn which essential oils should be used for the desired effect.

Powder, another safe substance for blessings and other magical charms, can be made by crushing the dry herb in a mortar and pestle until it resembles a fine dust. Roots and leaves can also be chopped fine by an electric coffee grinder that is set aside only for this use. Some people mix this herbal dust with an equal amount of unscented talcum powder while others say only the herb should be used.

Pure potpourri can also be utilized for magic. Potpourri can be made by combining the dry herb with a fixative and oil. Fixatives are what hold the scent in a potpourri. Good fixatives are powdered orris root, oak moss, or stag moss. I use oak moss because of its availability and price. You should be able to find fixatives in craft or herbal stores, while some health food stores also carry them. To make a potpourri, combine in a large jar: 1 cup of the herb, ½ cup of the fixative and 2 or 3 drops of the essential oil. Two or more herbs to be used for a similar purpose can be combined in one potpourri. Use your judgment when adding essential oil, and keep in mind that a few drops of each herb will usually be sufficient. Cap the jar tightly and shake daily for 5 days. Open and place in sachets. Potpourri can also be placed in open bowls to scent the room. To store your potpourri, place in airtight containers.

Incense can be purchased as cones, sticks, or blocks. However, the raw herb can also be smoldered on charcoal blocks within a container capable of holding red-hot coals. If someone in the house has allergies or asthma, it may be better to burn the raw herb. Place a few bricks of charcoal in a heat resistant container. A friend of mine has a metal pie pan nailed to a block of wood. The pie pan would burn a hole in the table if it was set directly on it. Light a few blocks of charcoal and let the flames die down. Get them red-hot and then carefully sprinkle your herbs over the top, not too much, just enough to scent the room.

The following table illustrates the desired effect and the different scents associated with particular substances. Some of these herbal scents are discussed in this book, and some are not. In fact, some of them aren't even herbs, but are rather plants and flowers. Consult individual chapters for more information.

Effect	Scent
Healing	Cedar, eucalyptus, lemon balm, thyme
Love	Jasmine, mint, rose
Luck	Heather, lemon balm, nutmeg
Money	Basil, chamomile, cinnamon, lemon balm
Peace	Chamomile, lavender, rosemary
Protection	Heather, rose geranium, basil

I was amazed to find that there are usually good reasons for a particular herb being used for a specific magical purpose.

An example of this would be the protective qualities of garlic when dealing with illness. Garlic has long been used as a healing herb, so it makes sense that it would be utilized in a healing or protection-from-illness charm.

Bathing in calendula is supposed to bring respect and admiration, as well as softening while stimulating the skin. Calendula can also make you feel more beautiful and in control of yourself, thus demanding more respect and admiration from those around you.

In each of these cases, I wouldn't go as far as to say that magical results are merely psychological: there is much more to it than that. But whatever the reason, herb magic can work for you.

You be the judge!

3
BASIL, THE
KING'S HERB

Basil is a relative of mint, with squarish stems growing to about two feet high. The leaves are one to two inches long and are oval, with teeth. They are usually dark green and slightly pointed at the end. Flowers appear in July or August on spikes and are white and purple.

As the herb used by European royalty for millennia, basil offers a regal touch to your garden even as it spices up the dishes you prepare for your table. A meal fit for a king, indeed!

Types of Basil

Sweet Basil—This is the most common culinary basil.

Lettuce Leaf Basil—This basil has large leaves and is excellent on salads.

Lemon Basil—Lemon scented basil grows twelve inches high with green leaves and white flowers. It is used in potpourri and in culinary dishes.

Bush/Greek Basil—This basil is small and compact with tiny green leaves. It grows about eight inches high.

Licorice Basil—Licorice basil has the distinctive scent and taste of licorice. Great in potpourri and cooking.

Cinnamon Basil—Cinnamon basil has the scent and flavor of cinnamon.

Holy Basil—This basil is very pungent and can be used in fruit dishes, jelly, and in potpourri.

Camphor Basil—This basil smells like camphor and is good for repelling moths and mosquitoes.

Opal Basil—Opal basil has purple leaves and lavender flowers. It has a mild basil flavor and can be used in cooking. Opal basil looks lovely in the flower garden.

Anise Basil—This basil has purplish leaves and has an anise flavor and scent.

Green Ruffles Basil—The leaves of this basil are crinkled and a lime green. This type of basil is only used ornamentally.

Purple Ruffles Basil—This basil has dark maroon, crinkled leaves. This is also an ornamental variety.

This list covers just a few varieties of basil. There are about 150 different types in all.

HISTORY, MAGIC, AND FOLKLORE

Basil has several other folk names, including American Dittany, Alabahaca, St. Joseph's Wort ("wort" is another word for herb, ultimately related to the word "root" in English), Sweet Basil, and Witches' Herb. This last folk name alludes to basil's extensive list of magical uses.

Basil is native to Africa, Asia, and India. In India it was a sacred herb dedicated to the gods Krishna and Vishnu. It was sprinkled around the house to protect the family, and sprigs were laid on the chests of the dead to protect their spirits from evil and give them safe passage into paradise.

The ancient Greeks and Romans used basil in exorcisms and purification rites. The word "*basileus*" is Greek for king, and basil must have been considered worthy of royalty, for it was used for royal oils and perfumes. More recently, the Greek Orthodox religion has used basil to prepare holy water.

Basil is also used in Greek villages to scare away the "*karkanzari*," creatures who are actually souls banished from heaven and whose purpose is to disturb the living. These ghostly beings haunt villagers and cause all sorts of mayhem during the twelve days of Christmas. During this time of the year, local priests come to each house in the community and perform blessings. They arrive bearing crosses wrapped in sprigs of basil and dipped in holy water; they enter each room in the house and bless it, sprinkling the basil and holy water as they go. As long as this ritual is carried out, the villagers believe their houses will be protected from the disturbances wrought by the *karkanzari*.

The herb was feared in medieval Italy, perhaps because of its powers. One superstition told that if one put a sprig of basil under a pot, it would turn into a scorpion; of course, it didn't help that these dangerous creatures love to rest under dark, moist pots. Basil received a bad reputation from this superstition, being associated as it was with scorpions. This is probably what gave rise to a legend about a man from Sienna who loved the pungent smell of basil so much he used it as a snuff. One day he was struck by a sudden madness and died; when his head was opened to find out what had killed him, a nest of scorpions was found in his brain.

This association with scorpions must have been ignored or forgotten later on, since another tradition tells of Italian women placing pots of basil on their balconies while preparing to receive their lovers.

Basil was widely used throughout Europe by the sixteenth century. In northern Europe, lovers would exchange sprigs of basil as a sign of faithfulness. Another legend says that if a man gives a woman a sprig of basil, she will fall in love with him and never leave. The exact opposite meaning is give the herb in other cultures, where basil became the symbol of hostility: in fact, gardeners in some regions were often heard shouting and cursing while planting basil seeds, a habit which gave rise to the expression "*semé le basilic*" ("sowing the seeds of basil"), a colloquial French term for ranting. Conversely, it is said that basil prevents drunkenness!

Traditionally, basil only grew in gardens of those that suffered great misfortune (I must have suffered greatly at some point in time merely because of the abundance of basil growing in my garden). Basil acquired the name "Witches' Herb" because its juice was combined in a potion that enabled witches to fly.

In the Victorian language of flowers, basil represents love and good wishes. This must be a reflection of its frequent use to create sympathy between two parties: its scent is said to hold off major clashes and create an atmosphere of understanding. It eases conflicts of both a personal and military nature: at root, basil creates harmony. Expanding on that characteristic, basil can be an integral part of any love potion or enchantment, and has been harnessed in charms of a sexual nature. Prostitutes in Spain, for instance, used to wear basil oil to attract business. The scent is said to stop quarrels between lovers. A gift of tea, oil, or incense is suitable to a wedding or anniversary couple. In fact, it's a good gift for anyone with whom you wish a more harmonious relationship. The powder can be sprinkled over your partner's heart to promote fidelity.

In Haiti basil was associated with a pagan love goddess, Erzulie. Two leaves placed on burning charcoal will foretell the nature of a relationship. If they crackle and spit the relationship will be querulous. If they fly apart, so will the people involved. If they lie quietly as they burn, the relationship will flourish in harmony.

Another quality of basil is to promote success: it can bring good luck. Wear the oil or carry a basil sachet when competing in any contests or competitions. Give a basil sachet to a hunter to ensure a successful quest. A Mexican practice was to carry basil in one's pockets, in order to attract luck and money. Because of this natural attraction, gamblers and treasure seekers should carry the herb with them. Basil is traditionally sprinkled around shops in Europe to provide protection and prosperity.

Basil augments purification rites. It can be used in ritual baths to purify body, mind, and soul and clear away any negativity. The scent is also useful as a meditational aid. An open bowl of basil, basil oil, or basil potpourri will dispel melancholy and negative energy.

For personal security, someone afraid of mischief or injury in a crowd should carry basil. This is part of basil's most common use, as a protective element in house blessings to bring peace, happiness, and prosperity to those who live in the home. The protective quality of the herb is used in exorcisms, where basil is strewn across the floor to protect those within its influence. Place a sachet in the highest point of the house or in each room for protection. Sprinkle basil powder into each of the four corners in each room of the house. Weave basil into a wreath and place it on the doors of the home or tie several sprigs of basil together with red ribbon and hang it. A pot of basil given as a housewarming gift will ensure luck in the new home. A sachet can also be placed under the driver's seat of the car to protect the driver and the passengers.

PROPAGATION AND CULTIVATION

Basil is an annual. This means it cannot withstand cold and will need to be replaced every year.

Basil grows easily from seeds, which can be planted outdoors after all danger of frost is past and the soil temperature reaches about 50 degrees. Plant seeds ⅛ inch deep. When the seedlings emerge, thin them using the following procedure: find the strongest and best-looking seedling, then pull all the rest out within a 1-foot area around your chosen plant. This insures "survival of the fittest" by encouraging the best seedling and giving it more room in which to grow.

Since consistent heat is necessary for growth, it is best to start basil indoors, especially if you live in a cold climate. Basil needs bottom heat to germinate. Place seed trays over heat (see chapter 1 for methods of propagation). Plant and cover with plastic. Germination should occur in three to seven days. Remove the plastic when several leaves open. Seven days after germination, transplant your seedlings into 2-inch pots or flats, containers, or plastic pop bottle bottoms.

This plant can be propagated by cuttings, but these rarely survive. Much better results come if you start from seed or purchase a plant from a nursery. Basil requires well-drained soil and a great deal of moisture: this is not a plant to grow during a drought.

Mulch around the plant to retain moisture. To mulch a plant, place a few handfuls of shredded bark, pine needles, or shredded newspaper around its base. Make sure this covers the earth all around the plant to about 2 to 3 inches deep. Mulch protects the plant by retaining moisture for longer periods of time. Also, you can mulch plants to "overwinter" them in cold climates, keeping them warm through the harsh months of winter.

Basil also requires full sun although it can be grown in partial shade. A shot of liquid fertilizer once in a while, even once a month, will keep your plant happy.

Do not allow basil to flower or it will not grow bigger. Once flower spikes begin to grow, pinch them off. This will encourage the plant to grow more leaves and branch out a little so it will be bushy.

Basil grows well in containers and makes a great border in your flower garden. Borders could consist of green and purple basil. Purple varieties look beautiful planted near the oranges, reds, and yellows of French marigolds or alongside the pinks and reds of dianthus, also called "pinks."

The growing requirements of basil and green peppers are the same, which means they can be grown near each other. Basil enhances the growth (and taste) of tomatoes and asparagus. The pungent smell keeps harmful insects away. Do not plant basil near rue. While basil is sweet, rue is bitter, and the plants will not grow near each other.

HARVEST

Leaves should be harvested while young. Harvest before flowering tops open. It is always best to harvest right after the morning dew has evaporated from the leaves. When you harvest, take about ⅓ of the length of the whole plant the first time, usually in midsummer (around mid-July). Between the end of August and the beginning of September, take another ⅓ of the plant. If you have a freeze in your, area make sure you pick everything that is left before the first frost. You can also pick leaves for your cooking pot at any time during the growth of the plant.

STORAGE

Basil leaves can be dried, frozen, or stored in oil.

Dried basil leaves tend to turn dark and ugly when dried by air. Remove leaves from their stems and place in a single layer on drying trays. It should take 4 to 10 days to dry. Basil bunches can also be hung upside-down to dry.

The microwave method is the best way to dry basil (see chapter 1). Remove leaves from their stems and place them between paper towels so they are not touching. Microwave on high for 1 minute. Continue at 30-second intervals until dry.

Store your dried basil in dark airtight jars or in resealable plastic bags. You can store them in regular clear jars but make sure you keep them in a dark place. They will keep longer that way. Never store near the stove where the heat can touch them. Heat will quickly dissipate the oils.

To freeze, paint both sides of the cleaned leaves with olive oil and place in freezer bags. You can tear leaves and place them in an ice cube tray partially filled with water. Freeze completely, pop cubes out of the tray, and store them in freezer bags, to be used later in soups and stews.

Put a cup of leaves in a food processor and add enough olive oil to make a paste. This will keep for a couple months in the refrigerator.

Culinary Uses

Basil lends a peppery flavor with just a trace of mint, cloves, or anise, and is most commonly used in Italian, Mediterranean, and Thai cooking. Store leaves in oil, vinegar, or as a frozen paste.

Always add basil at the last minute to cooked dishes so that the oil will not have time to evaporate. Tear basil leaves with your fingers when adding to salads.

The following recipes are easy ways to sample the taste of basil. Though this herb has a very strong taste, and many people don't like it, you should try a few of these dishes to see if basil is an herb for you.

Italian Seasoning

Prepare with all dried herbs and use in recipes requiring Italian seasoning.

> 5 tablespoons oregano
> 3 teaspoons basil
> 2 teaspoons parsley
> ½ teaspoon savory
> ½ teaspoon sweet marjoram

Perfect Pesto

This is my favorite pesto recipe because you can substitute walnuts or almonds for costly pine nuts.

> 1¼ cups fresh basil leaves
> 3 tablespoons pine nuts, walnuts, or almonds
> 4 tablespoons grated Parmesan cheese (fresh, please!)
> 3 cloves garlic
> Olive oil

Purée all ingredients in a food processor, adding enough olive oil to make a smooth paste while processing. If you are going to freeze the pesto, don't add the garlic. Garlic turns bitter when frozen. Instead, add garlic after defrosting your pesto.

Serve over fettucine noodles, or with chicken or fish. It tastes wonderful over cooked steak as well.

Pesto Pizza

We used to go to a little Italian restaurant all the time. I loved their
pasta with pesto sauce, while my husband loved their white pizza with
thin slices of tomatoes and no hot peppers. One day, we ordered our
regular dishes and the waitress tripped, upsetting her tray. About a third
of the pesto sauce ended up on the pizza, and a new dish was born.
After that night, the restaurant put it on their menu as "Tony and
Debbie's Pesto Pizza." Pesto gives a fresh flavor to pizza, a welcome
change from plain old tomato sauce. This is guaranteed to be a favorite.

Make a pesto pizza by spreading your pesto mixture on an oiled, uncooked pizza crust, then add tomato slices or hot peppers and a little bit of mozzarella cheese. Bake at 350 degrees until the crust browns and crisps, and the cheese melts.

Grilled, Basiled Veggie Mix

This can be made in the oven, but it's better when grilled outside. Use
it on a camping trip for a nutritious meal in the real outdoors.

Take a 10 x 10-inch square of foil and arrange sliced zucchini, onion, tomatoes, peppers, squash, and mushrooms. Add several basil leaves and fold foil tightly around all the vegetables. Grill for 20 minutes, flipping each package after 10 minutes. If you feel adventurous, add chunks of grilled beef top round or chicken.

Pesto Omelet

No chicken ever laid an egg like this!

2 tablespoons butter
2 tablespoons olive oil
6 eggs, separated
  Salt and pepper to taste
  Milk
  Tomato, sliced in thin rounds

Preheat an 8-inch iron frying pan over high heat (if you insist on making this dish in anything other than an iron pan, it won't taste the same). Melt butter and swirl in enough oil to coat the bottom of the pan. Separate yolks from whites of eggs in separate bowls. Beat whites to soft peaks. Beat yolks until frothy. Fold the whites into the yolks and pour into hot pan. Add salt and pepper. Let edges firm, then lift edges and allow liquid to flow underneath. Thin out pesto in a small bowl with a little bit of milk. When eggs are cooked through (edges will be firm and middle will be moist but not watery), remove from heat and spread thinned-out pesto on top. Add sliced tomato rounds and fold over. Serve immediately.

Basiled Bread

This bread has a strong basil flavor and will make your kitchen smell like an Italian cucina. Serve with basil butter (page 29).

3 cups self-rising flour
3 tablespoons sugar
1 can warm beer
¾ cup basil, chopped

Mix all ingredients and pour into a greased, 5 x 9-inch loaf pan. Do not preheat your oven. Instead, place pan in COLD oven and set temperature to 350 degrees. Bake 50 to 60 minutes until a toothpick inserted in center comes out clean. Remove from pan and cool on a wire rack.

Bouquet Garni

There are many recipes out there that require bouquet garni: here is how to make your own. Surprise, there's basil in it! Use all dried herbs.

4 teaspoons parsley
2 teaspoons rosemary
2 teaspoons sweet marjoram
1 teaspoon celery seed
4 teaspoons thyme
1½ teaspoons basil
2 teaspoons savory

Mix together and store in an airtight container to be used in recipes. (You can wrap several tablespoons in cheesecloth or coffee filters and tie to quickly throw in a pot.)

Basiled Eggs

This is another egg recipe that is good any time of the day.

6 eggs
¼ cup milk
⅛ cup crumbled dried basil or
¼ cup fresh chopped basil
2 tablespoons butter
⅛ teaspoon salt
   Pepper to taste
½ cup freshly grated Parmesan cheese
   Paprika (the Hungarian style is best)

Beat eggs, milk, and basil together. In a heavy frying pan, melt the butter. Add egg mixture and scramble. Sprinkle on salt, pepper, and cheese. Remove from heat. Cover with a lid and let sit until the cheese melts. Then sprinkle with paprika and serve.

Green Noodles

These are good served with chicken or fish.

8 ounces spinach noodles
¾ cup butter
2 tablespoons fresh basil

Cook spinach noodles per package instructions. Melt butter in a frying pan and add basil. Stir until basil wilts. Place cooked, drained noodles in a serving bowl and pour basil/butter mixture over top. Toss and serve.

Basil Butter

This is really good on hot homemade bread. It can also be used to sauté vegetables or stirred into pan juices for extra flavor in your gravy.

½ pound unsalted sweet butter
1 cup fresh basil, chopped

Soften butter to room temperature and cream with the back of a wood spoon. Blend in chopped basil. Form into a log and roll in more chopped basil. Wrap in waxed paper and refrigerate. When you use it, cut slices off the log.

Opal Basil Vinegar

With its pink color, this vinegar looks too pretty to actually use. It's great for gifts when presented in a clear bottle with a sprig of purple opal basil.

3 (3-inch) sprigs opal basil
White wine vinegar

Place sprigs of opal basil in a jar with white wine vinegar. In 2 or 3 days a pink color will be visible. Put jar in a sunny window for 2 or 3 weeks. Strain into a pretty bottle and add a chive blossom and a new sprig of opal basil. See chapter 13 for ways to use your vinegar.

Tomato Basil Salad

There aren't any quantities for this recipe because it depends on taste alone.

> Tomatoes, sliced into rounds
> Purple onion, or Vidalia onion, or
>   green onion, sliced
> Basil
> Olive oil in which several bruised cloves
>   of garlic have been steeping for
>   several days
> Parmesan cheese (optional)

Slice tomatoes and onions and place in a bowl or on a plate. Wash basil leaves and place on top of tomatoes and onions. Pour enough olive oil to coat and toss. Sprinkle Parmesan over top and enjoy.

Basil Jelly

A great combination with roast beef. Basil jelly is also yummy on crackers, with a little bit of soft cheese, like brie. Put a little bit in cottage cheese for a different flavor.

> 1½ cups packed basil
> 2 cups water
> 2 tablespoons rice vinegar or balsamic vinegar
>   Pinch of salt
> 3½ cups sugar
> 3 ounces liquid pectin

Chop basil in food processor and then place in a large saucepan. Add water, bring to a boil for 10 seconds, and remove from heat. Cover and steep 15 minutes. Strain. Pour 1½ cups of this liquid through a coffee filter or a fine strainer into another saucepan.

Add vinegar, salt, and sugar. Bring to a hard boil, stirring constantly. When boil can't be stirred down, add the pectin. Return to a hard boil and continue boiling for 1 minute. Remove from heat and skim foam. Pour into sterilized 8–ounce jars, leaving about 1½ inch headspace, and seal. Makes 4 8–ounce jars.

Basil Jelly II

Make apple jelly according to manufacturer's directions on powdered pectin. After skimming, divide mixture into 3 or 4 sterilized jars with 2 or 3 basil leaves placed inside them. Add food coloring if desired.

Stuffed Basil Tomatoes

Serve these on a hot day in the summer for a luncheon. It's sure to get many compliments.

- 4 large ripe tomatoes
- ¾ cup soft bread crumbs
- ½ cup fresh mozzarella
- ¼ cup chopped fresh basil
- 2 cloves garlic
- 1 tablespoon minced onion
- ¼ teaspoon salt
- ⅛ teaspoon pepper
- 5 tablespoons olive oil
- 3 tablespoons grated Parmesan cheese
    (fresh, not canned!)

Preheat oven to 350 degrees. Halve tomatoes and spoon pulp into a bowl. Place tomatoes, cut side down, on a paper towel to dry.

Combine bread crumbs, mozzarella, basil, garlic, onion, salt, pepper and 4 tablespoons of the olive oil with removed tomato pulp. Mix together well and pack into the tomato halves, which have been placed on a baking sheet. If the tomatoes don't sit upright you can cut off a tiny bit of the bottom to make them balance. Sprinkle tomatoes with Parmesan cheese and drizzle the remaining 1 tablespoon oil over top. Bake 20 minutes and serve.

Basil Tea

Even though this tea possesses many medicinal benefits, you can drink it just for the flavor. Enjoy some on a cold winter evening to get your circulation going.

> 6–8 sprigs any culinary variety of basil
> 4–6 cups rapidly boiling water

Place sprigs in a teapot and add boiling water to cover. Steep covered about 10 to 15 minutes. Strain. Add honey if desired.

REMEDIES

In all remedies, use sweet basil unless otherwise directed.

Basil is a particularly strong herb, and there are some cases where its use is not advised. Do not use basil internally if pregnant (see below for the reason why). Also, don't give basil infusions to children under ten years of age. A child's metabolism isn't as strong as an adult's, and there is a good chance that the very volatile oils in basil can exceed a child's physical tolerance; just taking a basil infusion orally could burn the inside of a young person's mouth. Better to find milder alternatives when treating children.

Indigestion—Use a regular infusion after a meal. This will aid digestion and dispel gas. Add basil to your food. It will prevent indigestion in some cases.

Stomach Cramps—An infusion of basil will help stomach cramps.

Anxiety—Basil has a slight sedative property, and an infusion will counteract nervous headaches and anxiety.

Constipation—Add a little chopped basil to a glass of wine and drink after a meal. Be careful with this remedy, though, because it can cause diarrhea as well.

Insomnia and Depression—A drop of basil oil on a pillow at night will help insomnia and depression. Use only a drop, since any more could be overpowering.

Sores—A poultice of basil seeds placed on sores aids in healing. Basil also has antibacterial properties.

Lung Congestion—A strong infusion of basil will help clear the lungs. When a cold has you really stuffed up, use for both your head and chest.

Nausea—An infusion is helpful when dealing with nausea, but do not use if you are pregnant. See the next tip for an explanation.

Menstrual Cycle—A strong infusion of basil can be taken to bring on the menstrual cycle.

Milk Production for Nursing Mothers—A strong infusion drunk several times a day will increase milk in nursing mothers. Use this ONLY after birthing is complete. Before childbirth, this treatment could bring on labor: please don't be impatient and use it to induce labor! The baby will come when it's ready and not before. Please don't do harm for the sake of hurrying along nature.

Acne—Use oil of basil on acne. Try a test spot on the underside of the arm first to see if any irritation occurs. If so, don't use the oil on your face.

Stings—A drop of basil oil can soothe a wasp sting. Crushed leaves of basil will stop a bee sting from swelling and aching. If you have extreme swelling or difficulty in breathing after being stung, seek medical help immediately. You might be allergic and in a potentially dangerous condition. Don't waste time trying herbal remedies in this situation: if you are seriously allergic, they won't work, and this is a matter of life and death.

AROMATIC USES

Basil has a sweet odor and smells exactly the same as it tastes. It is good in potpourri and sachets. Lemon basil is a wonderful addition to any citrus potpourri. Any of the purple basils look beautiful in potpourri.

A few drops of basil oil in a warm bath can refresh your spirits. It can relieve fatigue and nervousness as you sit in the scented water and breath in the fumes. But just to be safe, don't use basil in the bath if you are pregnant.

COSMETIC USES

Make an infusion and let cool. When washing your hair, do a final rinse with the infusion and do not rinse out. This treatment will really bring out the shine in your hair. You will, of course, smell a bit like pesto for a short while.

ORNAMENTAL USES

Basil gives flair to garden planters. Try planting purple basil with French marigolds: the colors are quite dramatic together. Purple basil makes an interesting border for a flower garden, while dried basil can be added to a kitchen wreath and either hung on the wall and just looked at, or used when you need a little basil. You can make an entire wreath of basil and hang it in the kitchen like a braid of garlic, for use in cooking. Just don't place it too close to the stove!

OTHER USES

Basil deters flies. Plant basil around your patio, near your doorways or place on your windowsill to keep flies away. Italian women suspend sprigs of basil over their heads while peeling tomatoes so that the flies wouldn't bother them.

Wipe down a plastic table cloth on an outdoor picnic table with a strong infusion of basil. This will keep the flies away. Keep a spray bottle handy with the infusion in it: if the flies begin to gather around your picnic table, just spray the table cloth with the infusion and they'll fly away.

4

CALENDULA, THE
CONSORT OF
THE SUN

Calendula looks like something that came directly out of our grandmother's gardens. The orange and yellow hue of this plant displays brightly in the garden.

The flower looks like a cross between a chrysanthemum and a daisy, in that the petals are fine and spidery. It also resembles the sunny head of a daisy with petals situated in rays around a central disc. About 1½ to 4 inches across, the flowers' colors run the gamut from light yellow to a deep orange. These flowers open wide at dawn and close up at night. The leaves are a pale green, oblong, with toothed edges. They are about 2 to 3 inches long. The plant stands about 12 to 18 inches tall and the stalk is covered in fine hairs.

Calendula is an annual, but usually reseeds itself profusely. Flowers appear in spring through the fall.

HISTORY, MAGIC, AND FOLKLORE

Calendula gets its name from the ancient Romans, who noticed that these bright flowers always seemed to open on the first day of every month (in Latin, "*calends*"). The Romans also used the flower heads to make a remedy for scorpion bites.

Calendula is also known as Marigold, Summer's Bredc, Husbandman's Dial, Holigold, Marybud, Bride of the Sun, Golds, and Gold. Another name for Calendula is Pot Marigold, not to be confused with the French Marigold found in many American gardens today.

One other name is Mary's Favorite Flower (i.e., "Mary's Gold"), which explains why some churches decorate their statues of the Virgin Mary with this flower. Fittingly enough, there is a legend that this was Mary's favorite flower, but there's no agreement among folklorists as to whether the story refers to the Virgin Mary or the seventeenth-century Mary Queen of Scots.

Anglo-American culture resounds with legends about the use of calendula. Before people were being burned in England for practicing witchcraft, a woman could determine if the man she loved was to become her husband by grinding calendula, marjoram, thyme, and wormwood into a fine powder. She would then simmer it in honey and wine and rub it on her body, afterward repeating this verse three times: "St. Luke, St. Luke, be kind to me/ In dreams let me my true love see." The woman would see the man in a dream: if he appeared kindly to her, he would make a loving husband; but if he seemed unkind, her husband-to-be would be disloyal. Milkmaids would put calendula petals in the churn to make their butter a golden color in England, and to this day, calendula is eaten as a vegetable.

Shakespeare has Friar Lawrence gather "goldies" in *Romeo and Juliet*. Its early name was *Spousa Solis* ("Spouse of the Sun") because it was said "she" sleeps with that celestial body; perhaps this refers to the fact that calendula flowers open at dawn and close at sunset. The seventeenth-century herbalist Culpepper, known for publishing herbal wisdom for the common people, called it "the Herb of the Sun" and linked it to the astrological sign of Leo, saying that it would strengthen the heart. Across the Atlantic, during the American Civil War calendula was used to stop bleeding and hasten the healing of wounds.

In general, these flowers are reputed to contain very powerful magic. Witness the belief that calendula can strip a witch of her powers. The flower signifies joy In the Victorian language of flowers.

If one drinks a concoction made from this flower, the tradition goes that they will be able to see fairies. A happy dream of a pot marigold foretells prosperity, riches, success, and a happy marriage. Also, according to legend, if calendula is picked at noon when the sun is strongest, it will comfort the heart. A young girl who touched the petals of calendula with her bare feet would supposedly be able to understand the speech of birds. Calendula was woven into wreaths or magical hoops (mandalas).

Carry a calendula sachet in your pocket when seeking a new job or a promotion. Calendula helps in legal matters, so carry a sachet when dealing with courts and lawyers. Calendula also helps put people at ease. Place a vase of the fresh flowers or add dried flowers in an open-bowl potpourri to create a congenial atmosphere and help to make all feel refreshed. Calendula in the bath will do wonders for the skin but it will also help the bather gain respect and admiration.

Calendula is helpful in matters of clairvoyance and prophetic dreams. To induce such dreams, stuff the petals in your mattress, or include them in a small dream pillow in or under your regular bed pillow. Another method is to place a sachet under your bed, or even scatter loose, dry petals: this should bring on prophetic dreams, and the scent will also give the sleeper peace and make their dreams come true.

Calendula is a protective herb. Combine with basil in a wreath and hang it on the doors to the home. It is said that this will prevent evil from entering the house. A power can also be made of the flowers and sprinkled into the four corners of each room of a house, or a sachet can be hung from the highest point in the house or in each room. Again, combine it with basil for best results. Calendula is often employed as protection from evil while spellcasting or performing sacred rituals. Many times the oil of Calendula is used in rituals during Beltane and to consecrate magical tools.

PROPAGATION AND CULTIVATION

Going somewhat against its "sunny disposition," calendula flourishes in dappled sunlight or partial shade. The plants will not tolerate intense heat, preferring instead mild or even cool temperatures. Sow the seed in any soil right after the soil can be worked. The only other care it needs is to be weeded and moderately thinned. Each plant should be separated by about 9 inches. Be sure to cut the flower heads for drying to encourage more flowering. Calendula will survive a light frost so they could be blooming all the way into October in the northern United States. They will reseed themselves if you leave some of the heads on the flowers. In fact, they'll reseed everywhere within their range, if you're not careful.

Calendula can come down with some diseases, such as leaf spot, stem rot, leaf blight, powdery mildew, and smut, among others. To prevent these, make sure your plants are no less than 6 inches apart from each other. This will ensure adequate air circulation, which in turn diminishes the threat of diseases.

The usual suspects from the insect world can threaten your plants, too. Slugs, snails, aphids, whiteflies, caterpillars, leaf hoppers, thrips, beetles and nematodes may hamper their growth. To rid your plants of harmful pests, make a bucket of soapy water and carefully pour this over your calendula, at least once a week, until the bugs are gone.

HARVEST

Harvest your calendula flowers as they open. Just pinch them off the stem. The foliage has no beneficial value.

STORAGE

Dry flower heads in the shade on newspaper. Don't use screens, since the petals tend to stick to them and make a mess. Pull petals off the dried head and store, or store the entire flower intact.

Store dry calendula in airtight jars. Any humidity can cause mold or rust on the petals.

CULINARY USES

Calendula isn't used widely as a culinary delight. As discussed in the history section, the English eat it boiled as a vegetable. There is one warning to diabetics about ingesting calendula: when taken internally it tends to dramatically lower the blood sugar, so diabetics should only use this plant externally.

One good culinary use for the dried flower head is as a substitute for saffron. It gives off a nice orange-yellow color as saffron does. The flowers may be added to stews, soups, or poultry dishes. They can also be added to salads to give a tangy flavor.

Make a calendula sandwich by mixing petals, sesame seeds, and mayonnaise, then spread on bread with cheese and liverwurst.

The following is another tasty calendula recipe.

Orange Calendula Drop Cookies

Make these up for something different to serve at luncheons or family gatherings. They have an unusual but pleasant flavor, and you can keep everyone guessing what the mystery ingredient is!

6–8 fresh calendula blossoms
¾ cup butter, room temperature
½ cup granulated sugar
Grated rind of 2 oranges
2 tablespoons orange juice, room temperature
(from the orange you grated)
1 teaspoon vanilla
2 eggs, lightly beaten
2 cups flour
2½ teaspoons baking powder
¼ teaspoon salt
1 cup almond halves

Preheat oven to 350 degrees. Rinse and pull off petals of flowers and set aside. In a bowl, cream butter, sugar, and orange rind until fluffy. Add orange juice and vanilla. Stir in eggs until well blended. Sift together flour, baking powder, and salt. Blend calendula petals and dry ingredients into the creamed mixture. Drop dough by teaspoonful onto a lightly greased cookie sheet. Press an almond half into each cookie. Bake 12 to 15 minutes, or until golden brown. Makes 3 to 4 dozen.

REMEDIES

Calendula can be used both internally and externally, except in the following cases: if you are pregnant, because it can be used to bring on menstruation; if you have high or low blood sugar, because calendula tends to lower blood sugar, sometimes too quickly and too low.

Refer to chapter 1 for information about preparing calendula in infusions, etc., and please see the medical disclaimer in the introduction of this book.

There are many other uses for this herb. Let's start with internal preparations.

Blood Circulation—Calendula can be used as a stimulant to increase blood circulation. Take an infusion twice a day.

Ulcers—Take an infusion twice a day to heal ulcers.

Digestion—Calendula can also increase the flow of bile and can be taken as an infusion to help ease digestive discomfort.

Menstruation—Take an infusion for painful menstrual cramps or to start a delayed period.

The external uses for this plant are numerous. Calendula provides a good antiseptic, and infusions can be used to heal and disinfect. Ointments can also be made to soothe soreness.

Cold Sores, Shingles, and Herpes—Dab an infusion on cold sores, shingles, or herpes. For shingles you may want to add a little St. John's wort.

Earache—Warm tea placed in the ear can ease the pain of an earache.

Sore Throat or Tonsillitis—Gargle with an infusion for sore throat. Use with chamomile added to treat tonsillitis and gargle every two hours alternating with hot lemon and honey drinks.

Tooth Extraction—After tooth extraction, gargle with an infusion for several days to prevent infection.

Fever—An infusion of the flower is good for a fever but do not use internally. Instead, soak up a warm infusion in a towel and place on the head. This promotes perspiration.

Varicose Veins—Mix 1 ounce calendula with 1 pint boiled water. Add ½ cup witch hazel and soak into a cloth to be placed on sore varicose veins.

Eczema and Psoriasis—Weeping and infected eczema can be calmed by a compress of a calendula infusion or a bath with a strong infusion added. This will also ease psoriasis.

Impetigo—Bathe affected area with a warm infusion and pat dry or a tincture can be used.

Ringworm and Athlete's Foot—Treat with a tincture applied directly to the area three times daily.

Eyestrain or Tired Eyes—Soak cotton balls in an infusion and apply to closed eyes for ten to fifteen minutes.

Sties—The pain of sties can be relieved with a warm compress of calendula infusion.

Acne—A cool infusion of calendula can be applied to the face to control acne. It tones the skin and closes the pores.

Bruises—A cold compress made with witch hazel and 1 teaspoon calendula will relieve the soreness of a bruise.

Burns and Cuts—An infusion can be used to heal minor burns or scalds and minor cuts and wounds.

Nosebleeds—Stop bleeding by holding cotton balls soaked in a calendula tincture to the nose.

Bleeding—An infusion held to a wound can stop the bleeding.

Sprains—Combine 1 pint boiling water to 5 tablespoons of petals and steep 30 minutes. Use as a compress for a sprain.

Vaginal Infections—Control by douching with an infusion or sitting in a shallow herb bath.

Sunburn—Bathe burned skin in a strong, cool infusion for relief.

Cracked Nipples (Nursing Mothers)—Soften and ease discomfort with a compress of an infusion right after feeding. This is non-toxic to the baby.

Stings—Rub a fresh flower on a bee sting to stop the pain and swelling.

Warts, Corns, and Calluses—Sap from the stem of calendula can remove warts, corns and calluses.

Calendula Ointment

A soothing ointment can be made from calendula flowers. It can be used to heal just about any skin condition such as minor cuts and scratches or burns. It will soften skin and heal chapped or psoriasis-affected hands. It also can be used for chillbanes (sores caused by exposure to cold).

Calendula petals
16 ounces olive oil
3 ounces beeswax

Macerate a few handfuls of calendula petals in olive oil and beeswax for a few hours over low heat in a double boiler. Press oil out through a muslin bag and pour while still warm into jars. A simpler method is to combine flower petals in olive oil and mix until goopy. To use, just apply to affected area. For affected hands or feet, apply at night and cover with white gloves or socks. This ointment can be used on chapped lips, but be careful not to lick it off if you have the dangerous conditions considered at the beginning of this section.

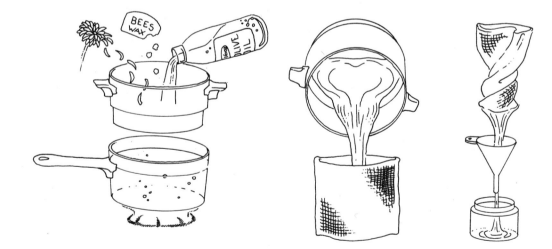

COSMETIC USES

As you can see, this herb is very useful. It also has many cosmetic uses.

A rinse for hair can be made from a strong infusion. This rinse will bring out the highlights in blond and brunette hair. To make a hair rinse combine 2 cups boiling water and 1 cup flowers. Let stand 30 minutes and strain. Rinse hair catching excess liquid in a basin and repeat 20 times. Let hair dry in the sun. This makes the hair shine.

Skin benefits from treatment with calendula. Soaking in an infusion can soften hands. Combine 1 cup of the flowers and leaves with 1 cup olive oil. Soak for several days then strain. Smooth on face at night for a soothing face cream.

A foot cream can be made by combining 1 cup fresh petals with ½ cup or 1 small jar of petroleum jelly. Place in a pan and heat on low for 30 minutes. Strain and store in a jar. Rub this cream on the feet at night and cover with socks. This will aid burning feet, sore feet, and calluses. You can use this on varicose veins too.

ORNAMENTAL USES

Calendula is very pretty in the garden. The colors run from a creamy pale yellow to a brilliant orange. The flowers fit in well with French marigolds, zinnias, or chrysanthemums. The dried petals of calendula look pretty in potpourri. Calendula will grow in containers but it also will reseed profusely.

OTHER USES

Calendula can be used as a dye. With the mordant alum and cream of tarter a pale yellow can be achieved.

Plant your calendula around evergreens to repel dogs. They don't seem to like the smell.

5

CHAMOMILE, THE GENTLE DOCTOR

The name of this herb can be spelled either chamomile or camomile. Chamomile's miniature daisy-like flowers, feathery leaves, and apple-like scent make it a favorite in any garden.

There are two different types of chamomile: Roman and German. Both have miniature daisy-like flowers with yellowish-orange centers and white to cream colored petals. The foliage is green, fine, and feathery.

German chamomile is an annual, and grows erect to about two or three feet. The flowers of this type smell vaguely of apples. It is used in remedies, in dyes, in pot-pourri, and even as insect repellent.

Roman chamomile is a perennial and grows to about four to twelve inches high. The foliage carries the plant's scent. In Europe it is used as ground cover. If mowed, it grows into a thick mat which, when walked upon, emits a strong apple scent. The Roman variety is best used as a hair rinse (especially for blondes), as an insect repellent, or in cosmetics. Both varieties bloom from May to October.

HISTORY, MAGIC, AND FOLKLORE

The folknames for chamomile include Maythen, Manzanilla, Chamalmelon, Cama-myle, Ground Apple, Earth Apple, and Whig Plant.

The flower of this herb represents the sun, as with calendula, because of its appearance. It is useful in unions and relationships of any type and is often used in love sachets.

According to legend, chamomile was one of the sacred herbs brought to the world by the Anglo-Saxon god Woden. Another legend tells that ancient Egyptians

dedicated chamomile to the sun. The reason for this was two-fold: the flower resembled the sun with its golden center and white rays, and it was also known for its power to cure chills and fevers, much as the streaming rays of the sun can.

Chamomile was used as a strewing herb in medieval England. The flowers were spread on the floor to freshen the air. Before the invention of refrigeration, meat was immersed in a chamomile infusion to prevent spoilage. In Spain the herb was used to flavor sherry.

When burned as an incense, chamomile will bring on an intense meditational state. It also induces a restful state and sleep when used this way, and is said to dispel nightmares.

The herb has an broad attracting property. Chamomile is used to bring prosperity to those who wear it on their person, allegedly "drawing money" to the wearer; this leads to tales of gamblers using an infusion to wash their hands before a game, in order to attract money. An infusion can be added to the bath to attract love.

General protections can also be cast using chamomile. Based on its historical use as a strewing herb, it can be scattered around property and individuals to remove curses. The herb is sometimes planted in the garden to protect against evil and can be included in amulets to bring success.

Chamomile has been called "The Plant Physician" because a dying plant placed near it will recover. In the Victorian language of flowers, chamomile means "humility" or "may all your wishes come true."

PROPAGATION & CULTIVATION

Chamomile is an annual, but it reseeds itself so you don't generally have to replant it every year. Chamomile can be grown in full to partial shade to full sun in just about any type of soil. Chamomile grows wild in fields, along roads, and on embankments. The seed is very fine and must be planted in very light soil. Sow outside in the spring by scattering seed and pressing lightly into the soil. Do not cover seeds with soil. Plants from the nursery can be planted (in early spring) after all danger of frost is over. Divide established plants in the spring as well. German chamomile can also be planted in the fall in regions with moderate climates; Roman chamomile is best propagated by root division in the spring. Both types of chamomile will reseed themselves. In fact, it will probably come up where you don't want it, since the seed is so light it can be carried by the wind just about anywhere.

Chamomile doesn't do particularly well in containers. It tends to grow tall and lanky, and does better if it can be grown directly in the ground.

HARVEST

Harvest the flowers when the petals begin to turn back on the yellow disk. This can be done at any time during the growing season.

Storage

Place the flowers in a tightly woven basket and hang to dry. It will only take a few days to a week for them to dry. The petals will generally fall off, leaving the yellow mounded center and a pile of dust.

Culinary Uses

There aren't very many culinary uses for this herb, but the taste of this jelly is very delicate and quite pleasing to the palate.

Chamomile Jelly

A great combination of flavors with roast lamb or pork, this jelly brings out a crisp apple nuance. Another way to serve is with crackers and soft cheeses, or on crackers all by itself.

> 1 cup chamomile flowers
> 3½ cups water
> 1 box powdered pectin
> 4½ cups granulated sugar

Place chamomile in a medium pan, add water, and bring to a rolling boil. Remove from heat, cover, and let stand for 15 to 20 minutes. Strain through cheesecloth or a coffee filter. Place liquid in a 4-cup measuring cup. You should have about 3 cups of liquid. If you don't, add more water to make 3 cups. If you have a little more liquid than desired, either save it for your next batch or throw it away. Mix your liquid with powdered pectin in a large saucepan. Bring to a rolling boil and add sugar. Bring to another rolling boil and boil 1 minute, stirring constantly. Remove from heat and skim the foam from the top. Pour into hot sterilized jars and seal. You will get anywhere from 3 to 4 pints, or else you can use small jelly jars. You can get 6 to 8 of those sealed with paraffin.

REMEDIES

Either variety of chamomile can be used for remedies, but German chamomile is most commonly used. As with many other herbs described here, do not use chamomile internally if you are pregnant. Also, don't use it in any way if you are allergic to ragweed: chamomile will only aggravate your allergy. Use of this herb for more than one week is not advised.

See chapter 1 for information on preparing infusions, etc., and please see the introduction for a medical disclaimer.

Chamomile is an anti-inflammatory (i.e., it eases the pain caused by inflammation), and an antispasmodic (i.e., helps to relax muscles, aids in digestion, dispels cramps, etc.).

Infusions of this herb are helpful in relieving many maladies. Make a regular infusion for the following.

According to tradition, chamomile can be used to relieve allergies, but since it also seems to cause many allergic reactions itself, it is not wise to use it for this purpose.

Insomnia—Drink 1 cup hot infusion before bed. This will relax the body and induce sleep.

Indigestion—Drink 1 cup hot infusion before or after a meal, or when first signs of indigestion appear.

Headaches—Drink 1 cup hot infusion at first sign of a headache. You may sweeten the infusion with honey if desired.

Kidney or Bladder Infections—Drink 1 cup hot infusion three times daily. This will force the toxins out that are causing the infection.

Colitis—Drink 1 or 2 cups of a strong infusion at onset of discomfort.

Menstruation—Sip a warm, strong infusion as long as it takes to relieve pain. This will also promote menstruation.

Nausea and Vomiting—Sip warm tea. DO NOT USE FOR MORNING SICKNESS: chamomile is used to start menstruation and can be dangerous to the fetus.

Warts—Warts appear because there is too much lime in the body. To neutralize this condition, drink a strong infusion: 1 cup, two to three times per day.

Chapped Skin—Use a cooled infusion by dabbing on the affected area and letting it air dry.

Pinkeye—Use a cooled infusion as an eyewash to ease the symptoms of pinkeye. Soak up in a cloth and use as a compress. Make sure you disinfect the cloth or throw it away after each use, as pinkeye is very contagious and you can reinfect yourself if not careful.

Eyestrain or Tired Eyes—Soothe tired, aching eyes by soaking chamomile tea bags in ice water and apply to the eyes. Make your own tea bag by cutting out the circle at the bottom of a coffee filter, place the chamomile in the center and bring up all the edges to make pouch, tying it off with a piece of string.

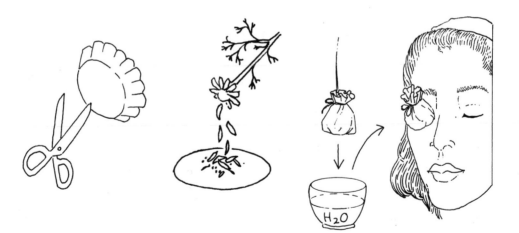

Depression—Place a handful of flowers in a coffee filter and rubber-band it shut. Throw it in a warm bath before bathing. This will also help relax tense, tired muscles.

Diaper Rash—Boil 1½ cups water and 1½ tablespoons chamomile flowers. Cover and steep until cool. Strain. Add 3 teaspoons cod-liver oil to the liquid. Shake well and apply to the affected area.

COSMETIC USES

Chamomile is good in many cosmetic applications for hair, skin, and eyes.

For Hair

Combine 1 ounce fresh ground ginger (you can buy this in the produce section of your grocery store; buy the root—don't use the ground ginger that comes in a can or jar) and 1 ounce chamomile flowers in a cheesecloth or coffee filter. Tie off. Place in 1 gallon of water. Bring to a boil and let boil 10 minutes. Cool and pour into a bottle. After shampooing, massage a small amount of this mixture into your hair and style. Do not rinse out. This acts as a conditioner and will bring out highlights in the hair.

For a hair rinse, boil 5 cups of water and add 2½ tablespoons flowers. Remove water from heat and steep covered until cool, then strain. Rinse over hair, catching excess liquid in a bowl, and re-rinse at least twenty times. DO NOT RINSE OUT WITH WATER. This treatment lightens hair, giving gold highlights to brown hair, while it brings out the shine in blond hair: in general, this rinse promotes hair growth.

A shampoo can be made by combining 5 cups boiled water with 1 cup flowers. Steep covered for 30 minutes, strain and add 5 ounces castile soap flakes. This shampoo will not lather like commercial ones but it cleans very well. Castile soap can be purchased at most pharmacies and health food stores, as well as from some craft stores.

For Skin and Eyes

Apply a regular infusion to chapped skin and lips. Let air-dry.

Steam your face clean by adding 4 tablespoons chamomile flowers to 4 cups water. Bring to a boil and remove from the stove, placing the pot on a hot pad on a counter or table. Place a towel over your head and the pan for about five to ten minutes. Be careful not to burn yourself. Let skin air-dry.

To tone and relax muscles, make a strong infusion. Bottle and refrigerate. Dab cold solution on face and body. This will keep for about one week in the refrigerator.

To remove calluses on feet, make a strong infusion and soak feet in it for 10 to 20 minutes. The calluses will peel right off. This process will stain the skin, so make sure you rinse the solution off well.

Puffy eyes can be eased by applying chamomile tea bags soaked in cold water.

AROMATIC USES

Chamomile has the pleasing scent of apples and can be used in potpourri.

Chamomile and Rose Potpourri

This potpourri has a lovely scent for any living space or a bath area.

      1 cup dry rose petals (preferably pink)
      ½ cup dry chamomile flowers
      ½ cup dry rose geranium leaves
      ½ cup orris root
    4–5 drops rose oil

Mix together and add pieces of ½ to 1-inch-wide pink or yellow ribbon cut in 1-inch lengths. You can also add dried rose buds.

Chamomile and Spice Potpourri

This potpourri is good in the kitchen, lending a homey atmosphere with a scent of baked goods. When a woman I know was selling her house, she set this potpourri out in her kitchen and the house sold in a matter of days.

1 cup dried chamomile flowers
1 cup dried nutmeg-scented geranium leaves
1 cup dried apple peel
½ cup orris root
2 tablespoons cinnamon
3 drops nutmeg, cinnamon or
   other spice-scented oil
3 drops apple-scented oil

Mix together and add a few whole nutmeg seeds and small pine cones or cinnamon sticks.

OTHER USES

Chamomile will enhance the growth of any plant it is placed near, but it especially enhances the growth of cucumbers and onions.

Roman chamomile is also called Dyers' Chamomile. Flowers mixed with alum will yield a golden color, while flowers combined with chrome yield a pale yellow. German chamomile can also be used as a dye, but it gives a lighter, more delicate shade.

A strong infusion applied in the bathtub or shower stall will get rid of mildew.

6
CHIVES, A TASTE FROM THE ORIENT

Chives are a perennial, which means that the plant returns year after year. They grow from bulbs that are clustered together. The leaves are cylindrical, hollow, and green in color, resembling thick blades of grass. Chives grow up in fountain-like tufts and reach a height of twelve to sixteen inches. Established plants will begin to pop up after the weather begins to warm in the spring. If a cold snap hits, your chives will appear to be dead, but give them time: they'll come back again once it warms up.

55

The flowers come in several colors, but the most common is a purplish pink or white. Occasionally you will see white, yellow, or lavender and pink flowers, too. They look like pompoms and grow on tall stems that are taller than the leaves. The plant usually flowers in June and July.

There are different varieties of chives. Most have green leaves, but some have bluish ones.

HISTORY, MAGIC, AND FOLKLORE

The cultivation of chives began about 5,000 years ago in Asia and the Middle East where the plant was used to season food. Marco Polo is said to have taken the herb back with him and introduced it to Europe, and medieval Greeks were familiar with it (probably from the influence of the Ottoman Empire in Turkey). The herb appeared widely in the West by the sixteenth century. It was brought to America in the first waves of European colonization.

Owing to its late introduction to the West, there isn't much folklore related to this herb, nor does it seem to have been used for magic. Bunches of chives were hung in central European homes to keep away evil, and Romanian gypsies have traditionally told fortunes with the plant's leaves.

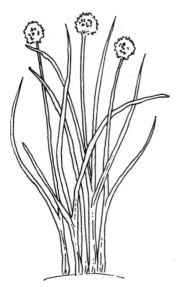

PROPAGATION AND CULTIVATION

Chive seeds germinate very slowly and require total darkness, constant moisture, and temperatures in the 60s to the 70s. In that light (or lack thereof), it is much better to deal with an established plant than to try starting seeds.

Either purchase plants or divide established plants in the springtime, planting clumps of 3 to 6 bulbs, 5 to 8 inches apart in a sunny, well-drained area. Plants need to be divided every three years to avoid letting them grow too big.

Chives will produce a blossom in the late spring. It will be white, cream, mauve, or purple in color and extend above the plant on its own erect stem. As already mentioned, the flower resembles a pompom; these blossoms must be cut in order to promote the growth of leaves, which are used in many applications. The flowers are edible, delicious in salads and other dishes.

Chives can be successfully grown in containers during the summer or they can be transplanted into pots and brought in for the winter. Chives do need a cold period, however. When the plant begins to die back and turn brown or yellow, place the pot outside in a protected area and leave there until the roots freeze. Do not bring inside for three or four weeks. When the plant is brought in and warmed, it will begin to send out leaves. Place in a sunny spot and you will have a full plant in just a few weeks.

Being a perennial, chives tolerate partial shade, though they prefer full sun. They also tolerate poor soil, which means they will grow well in whatever soil you happen to plant them in. Chives bloom from May to June. Once the weather becomes very hot, chives stop blooming.

HARVEST

Snip off leaves any time after the plant has reached 6 inches tall. Don't cut all the way to the ground. Leave about 2 inches for regrowth. Make sure you snip the flowers, too, and save them. You can leave a few on for show if you like. Cut back 3 or 4 times during the growing season and give a slight haircut at least 2 times a month. I have found that regular cutting for use in the kitchen is good enough to keep your supply of chives up and to encourage your plant to grow more.

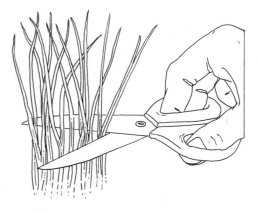

STORAGE

Place cuttings in plastic storage bags and refrigerate up to 7 days. Cuttings can also be frozen in bags or chopped up and placed in ice cube trays with water to freeze. Pop out the cubes and store in a freezer bag. Take one or two cubes and throw in soups or stews when needed. Place cuttings in baskets to dry, then place in airtight jars for storage.

CULINARY USES

Chives have a mild oniony taste and the flowers are edible. Some varieties taste like a combination of chives and garlic. They are good on any salad (as are the flowers), in soups and stews. Try putting some snipped chives on a baked potato or in mashed potatoes. Use on chicken, fish, or egg dishes. Chives also give zip to ordinary cottage cheese. Snipped chives can be used as a garnish on tomato or other smooth, dark soups: they look wonderful floating on top. Chives can be used fresh, frozen, or dried.

The following are a few good recipes for using this herb.

Garlic and Chive Cheese Spread

There won't be any leftovers when you serve this appetizer. Make a big batch and give as gifts in decorative stoneware jars.

> 2 cloves garlic
> Pinch of salt
> 1 tablespoon chopped parsley
> 2 tablespoons snipped chives
> 1 cup cream cheese
> Pepper to taste

Peel garlic, place cloves in enough boiling water to cover, and cook partially (i.e., blanch). It should be ready after 3 minutes, when the cloves should be crisp, not mushy. Crush garlic clove in a dish with a pinch of salt. Beat garlic and herbs into the cream cheese. Add pepper to taste. Chill and serve with crackers.

Cheese Balls

These are delectable on hot bread.

> Chives
> Parsley
> Rosemary
> Sage
> Thyme
> 8 ounces cream cheese

Combine chopped herbs to make 1 cup. Shape cheese into small balls and roll in chopped herbs. Serve as a spread for crackers or specialty breads.

Parsley Chive Butter

Serve this on any type of crusty bread to get a mild, oniony flavor.

> 2 tablespoons chopped parsley
> 1 tablespoon snipped chives
> 8 ounces softened butter
> Juice of 1 lemon
> Salt and pepper to taste

Beat herbs into butter with a spoon or fork and add lemon juice. Mix until smooth. Chill. Shape in a mold or roll into little balls. These can be frozen and tastes quite lovely on Chivey Cheese Bread (page 60).

Chivey Cheese Bread

Serve this bread with spaghetti or any other Italian dish.

1 ounce dried yeast
1 teaspoon sugar
¼ cup water
3½ cups all-purpose flour
¾ cup whole-wheat flour
   Pinch of salt
1 cup warm water
3 ounces butter
2¼ cups cheese, grated
   (use fresh Parmesan—not
   canned—or cheddar)
3 tablespoons chopped chives
1 egg, beaten

Stir ¼ cup water into yeast and sugar. Leave in a warm place until it gets frothy. Place both types of flour in a large bowl. Pour yeast mixture into the center of the flour and mix with a knife, adding more of the warm water until all is used, then knead for 2 minutes. Form dough into a ball, sprinkle with flour, cover with a damp cloth, and leave to rise in a warm place. When the dough has doubled (1½ to 2 hours later), knead lightly. Roll into a rectangle and dot with butter. Fold over and roll out again. Sprinkle with cheese to within 1 inch of the dough's edge. Roll up from the short end like a jelly roll. Place in a greased pan and score top. Leave in a warm place for 30 minutes, allowing it to rise again.

Preheat oven to 425 degrees. Brush top of loaf with a beaten egg and bake for 35 to 40 minutes.

Fiddlehead Fern Salad

This is a little unusual, but if you can find the ingredients, it's well worth trying.

> 1 cup steamed fiddlehead fern
> ½ cup watercress tips
> 1 cup white or purple violet leaves and flowers
> ½ cup snipped chives

Dressing

> ¼ cup cider vinegar (balsamic gives
>   a different taste)
> 2½ tablespoons honey
> ⅛ teaspoon salt
> ⅓ cup vegetable oil (olive oil tends
>   to be a little strong for this)

Blend dressing ingredients thoroughly and toss with greens. Garnish with leaves and flowers.

REMEDIES

Chives contain a high amount of iron, but there really aren't that many remedies using chives.

Refer to chapter 1 for information about preparing chives in infusions, etc., and please see the medical disclaimer on the copyright page of this book.

Here are a few that don't require any special preparation. In all treatments, use the snipped herb.

Appetite Stimulant—Sprinkle chives on the appropriate food to boost appetite.

Digestion—Chives promotes digestion when eaten in their natural form.

Blood Pressure—An old folk remedy claims that chives lower blood pressure, perhaps because they are high in sulfur.

ORNAMENTAL USES

Chives dry well and look attractive in arrangements and wreaths. Their flowers will usually retain color when dry.

Chives also make a nice border in the garden, since they can grow quite thick.

OTHER USES

Grow chives near carrots, as they will enhance the vegetable's flavor. They are also beneficial to grapes, roses, and tomatoes. Chives deter Japanese beetles and aphids, and they can also prevent scabbing on apples.

Make an infusion of chives, let sit overnight, strain, and add 2 times the amount of water. Spray on roses 3 times in a day, then after a heavy rain to prevent black spot and to get rid of aphids.

A strong infusion of chives can rid the bathroom and basement of mildew. Store the excess in the refrigerator.

Dried chives also repel moths.

7

GARLIC, AN ALLY IN THE FIGHT AGAINST ILLNESS

Garlic appears in cooking as a bulb enclosed in a papery sack, also referred to as the "head." Each bulb is made up of 4 to 15 cloves, which are also encased in a papery white substance: this must be peeled before using the cloves.

Leaves of garlic rise from the plant's base up to about 2 feet and are about half an inch wide. They resemble large, flat chive leaves or grass. The flowers are on a stalk and are very small, ranging in color from white to purple. They bloom in June and July.

Garlic is an annual, so it must be planted every year. A member of the onion family and a relative of the lily, it is also known as the Stinking Rose, Heal-all, or Poor Man's Treacle.

HISTORY, MAGIC, AND FOLKLORE

Because of the antiquity of the plant, it is hard to calculate how long garlic has been used and cultivated. Traces of garlic have been found in caves that were inhabited over 10,000 years ago, so it is safe to say that humans have been using garlic for most of their history on earth.

Egyptians swore oaths on garlic, and they fed their slaves garlic to give them strength and endurance while they were building the pyramids. At one point in time, garlic was withheld from the slaves: their immediate response was refusal to work, causing one of the earliest labor strikes known to man. That the pyramids were completed is testimony to its power. After their pyramid-building period, Egyptians must have still revered garlic, since it was left in King Tut's tomb as an essential plant for the afterlife.

The other great powers of the ancient Mediterranean respected garlic, too. From ancient Greece comes the legend that if one chews garlic during a foot race, no one will be able to match the runner in swiftness. Later, the Romans called garlic the herb of Mars, the god of war, since it was supposed to supply strength and bravery. They would eat garlic before battle to ensure courage, much the same as the earlier pyramid-builders of Egypt had taken it for strength.

A medieval French legend tells of "Four Thieves Vinegar." The story goes that four thieves were employed to bury the victims of the plague in Marseilles. They never became ill because they drank a mixture of crushed garlic and wine vinegar. This remedy has been sold in France since the eighteenth century (and no one has died of the plague since). Another legend concerns the creation of garlic: when Satan stepped into the world, garlic sprang from his left footsteps while onion grew from his right.

In Italy a clove of garlic was bitten when someone felt the presence of evil spirits: this would banish the spirits. A sachet incorporating garlic, hung by a red thread from the walls and doors or included in a protective wreath, was traditionally used to protect a home.

In magical practice, garlic possesses power against evil and is used to cast spells or charms. In some areas of Europe, braids of garlic are hung by doors to keep evil entities out. Newborns are presented with garlic to guard against the evil eye; to protect adults, a bulb of garlic is threaded on a piece of red yarn and worn around the neck for a time. Garlic allegedly protects against shipwrecks and drowning. Since it prevents storms at sea, it should be taken along on trips over water. And, as a preventative against storms on land, mountain climbers have been known to carry garlic with them to ensure fair weather.

Garlic is ruled by Mars, which lends it the ability to battle illness. Cloves of garlic can be placed in each room of a house when illness threatens its occupants, or a string of garlic bulbs can be hung on the wall in each bedroom to ward off disease. There is good reason for this. Both onions and garlic have a tendency to attract germs, so that the germs are attracted to the "fruit" instead of to the people in the house. That is why you should never leave a peeled or cut garlic clove out, uncovered, and then use it: it works like a magnet to collect germs.

Many different folkloric traditions hold that garlic will absorb disease if the cloves are rubbed on an affected part of a sick person's body. The clove must be thrown into running water immediately afterwards in order for this treatment to work. Some people rub garlic on their cooking pots to keep negative vibrations away from their food. Garlic has also been traditionally used in foods to induce lust, which seems pretty unusual in light of the scent it produces.

Garlic is used in exorcisms and purifications. For these rituals, peeled cloves are placed on the floor in the center of each room in a house. After a purification ritual has been performed by a practitioner, the cloves are gathered without letting them touch skin and then immediately thrown away. It is important that the practitioner not touch the "used" cloves, as the negative

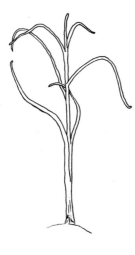

influences will have been absorbed into the garlic and can be transferred to another person.

Garlic is said to repel vampires, and no wonder: would you bite someone's neck if they reeked of garlic? Vampires are supposedly frightened away by garlic, and whether it is the scent or the sight of the stuff, who cares, just as long as it works! Braid 3 garlic stalks together with the bulbs at the base. Take the end of the braid and bend around toward the bulbs making a loop and hang on a nail by the door. These braids are said to guard against any type of evil and are thought to frighten away thieves, turn away the envious, and bring good blessings to new homes.

See the Remedies section below for more historical and traditional uses of garlic.

PROPAGATION & CULTIVATION

Start garlic from cloves. Garlic grown from someone's garden can be used as well as any garlic purchased from the grocery store. It can be planted in the early spring (up to 6 weeks before the last frost) for a fall harvest, but the best way to cultivate garlic is to plant it in late fall to harvest in the following summer. Snow and cold will not cause harm to the clove. We plant in October and harvest in late July or early August. This way the roots have a chance to grow and establish themselves before the ground freezes.

Plant individual cloves (not heads). Pull them apart and leave the papery skin on. Plant with the pointed end up about 2 inches deep and 1 foot apart in full sun, although garlic will also tolerate partial shade. Do not allow to blossom. When flower stalks appear cut them off or knock the stalk over, breaking it at the base. If it does flower, the strength of the plant will not go to the roots underneath the ground and you will end up with small cloves, or no cloves at all.

Harvest

When the leaves of garlic begin to yellow and brown, they are ready to pick. If this doesn't happen by midsummer, knock the leaves and stalks down until they do turn brown. Pull from the ground and place on a screen or on newspaper in the shade to dry.

Storage

Garlic should be stored in a cool, dark place. One storage method is to place garlic heads in mesh bags (potato or onion bags). Garlic can also be braided and hung.

To braid, do not cut the leaves from the heads. Keep intact and let dry somewhat. Take 3 large heads and arrange as shown in the illustration below left. Braid the leaves together twice, close to the heads, so that leaves don't show between. Add a fourth head above the center one and braid, as in the illustration below right. Add 2 more heads, this time to each side of the center and braid.

Add another in the middle, then two at the sides and so on until you run out of garlic. Tie the end with twine to hang and dry.

Garlic can also be separated from the head, with the skin removed, and placed in a jar of olive oil. This will keep refrigerated for about 3 months.

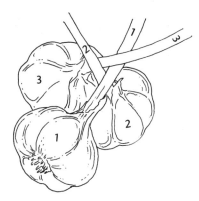 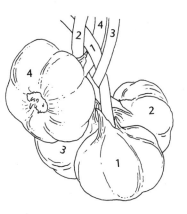

Culinary Uses

Garlic is used in Mediterranean and Eastern Cuisine. When one considers garlic, they automatically think Italian food.

One thing must be made clear when cooking with garlic: the clove is the individual meat from a head of garlic; think of the clove as the smallest unit of measurement. When a recipe calls for 1, 2, or more cloves, it isn't talking about the large, multicloved head. We knew two young men who decided to make a recipe calling for three cloves of garlic. They used three heads and ended up having to fight over the bathroom for the next few days. Powerful stuff!

Here are some other tips to keep in mind.

Garlic becomes bitter if burned.

Garlic can become bitter if frozen.

To peel, squash a clove with the flat of a knife first.

You can get garlic in several different forms: fresh, dried, flakes, powder, or in oil.

Rub a clove of garlic around a salad bowl (wooden bowl is most desirable) for flavor.

Insert pieces of garlic in meat before roasting.

Garlic vinegar can be used as a base for salad dressings or in marinades for meats.

To get the smell of garlic off your hands, rub with lemon juice.

Here are a few recipes that will keep the vampires away and keep you gastronomically content.

Garlic Butter

Serve this on warm Italian bread to get those taste buds excited.

>   1 cup softened butter or margarine
>   (butter works better)
>   4 small cloves of garlic, crushed

Beat all together in a small bowl, then process in the mixer at high speed until fluffy and light. Refrigerate in a covered container and use for up to 1 week. Use on hot rice, warm bread or rolls, hot vegetables, or on broiled steak.

Garlic Soup

Soup for the true garlic lover. It has a rich flavor that the die-hards will want again and again.

>   5 cloves garlic
>   1 tablespoon olive oil
>   1 quart beef stock
>   2 eggs, separated
>   2 tablespoons vinegar
>   Salt and pepper to taste
>   Croutons

Cut up garlic and sauté in the oil, be careful not to burn because it will become bitter. Add the stock and let boil for five minutes. Lower heat. Separate eggs and add whites to the hot liquid, stirring rapidly. I find a metal whisk to be the best implement to use. Combine yolks with vinegar and pour into the soup. Add salt and pepper. Ladle into individual bowls and add a few croutons to float on top.

Marinara Sauce

This is thinner than spaghetti sauce, and works well over regular spaghetti pasta. Try it over rigatoni or bow ties for added flare.

> 6 large garlic cloves, chopped
> ⅜ cup olive oil
> 1 (28-ounce) can crushed tomatoes
> 28 ounces water (use the empty tomato can for a measure)
> 1 tablespoon salt
> ½ teaspoon pepper
> ¾ teaspoon parsley flakes
> ½ teaspoon basil
> 1 teaspoon crushed red pepper
> Dash of garlic powder
> 1 pound thin spaghetti

Sauté garlic in the oil and lightly brown, but don't burn or it will taste bitter. Add tomatoes, water, salt, pepper, parsley, basil, red pepper, and garlic powder. Cook in a pot, uncovered, for 30 minutes stirring often. Meanwhile, cook the spaghetti according to package directions and drain. Place spaghetti on a platter or in a large bowl and pour sauce over top and serve.

Babaganoush

My husband and neighbor love this, but you can't get near to them for several days after they've eaten it.

>   2 large eggplants
>   ¼ cup olive oil
>   Juice of 1 medium-sized lemon
>   3 cloves garlic, crushed
>   Salt and pepper to taste

Preheat oven to 350 degrees. With a fork, puncture the eggplants in several places (if you don't puncture the eggplants, they'll explode and make a real mess in your oven). Place on a baking sheet covered with foil and bake for 1 hour or until soft. Remove from oven and cool. Cut eggplants open and scoop the insides out. Chop the insides finely and place in a bowl. Mix in oil, lemon juice, garlic, and salt and pepper. Serve in a small bowl with crackers, toast, or torn pita bread slices.

Old-Fashioned Garlic Bread

You'll never buy frozen garlic bread again once you've tried this recipe.

>   1 loaf French bread (you can use
>   Italian, but French is denser
>   and works better)
>   2 cloves garlic
>   ½ teaspoon salt
>   6 tablespoons butter

Preheat oven to 400 degrees. Make wide diagonal cuts in the bread but don't cut all the way through. Peel garlic, crush, and mix with salt. Add this mixture to the butter, beating until smooth. Spread butter on each side of a slice of bread, then squeeze back together and spread remaining butter over the crust. Wrap the loaf in foil and bake 10 to 15 minutes in preheated oven.

Garlic Oil

Cook everything you can think of in this oil in place of regular olive oil.
The difference in taste will be astounding.

3 large cloves garlic
1½ cups olive oil

Crush garlic and place in jar with olive oil. Leave in the jar for 2 weeks, shaking the jar daily. Strain. If oil has a garlic scent, it's ready to use. If not, place 3 more crushed cloves of garlic in the oil and set aside for another week, shaking daily.

Basil-Garlic Vinegar

Adding this vinegar to your favorite salad dressing recipe will enhance any salad.

1 clove garlic
10 tablespoons chopped basil
2 cups white wine vinegar

Peel garlic, chop, and crush. Add chopped basil leaves and crush again. Heat half of the vinegar and pour while boiling over the herbs. Pound. Leave to cool. Mix with unheated vinegar and pour into a bottle. Keep 2 weeks, shaking every few days. Strain and rebottle.

Garlic Omelet

What a way to wake up in the morning! Eggs never tasted better than with garlic added to them.

2 slices dry bread
1 large clove garlic
¼ cup butter
5 eggs
   Salt and pepper to taste
½ tablespoon finely chopped parsley

Trim crusts from bread and cut into cubes. Peel and crush garlic. Heat most of the butter in a frying pan, enough to leave a coating on the bottom. Fry bread until golden and add crushed garlic. Remove from pan and set aside. Break eggs in a bowl and season with salt and pepper. Heat remaining butter in an omelet pan (if you don't have one a skillet is fine) and add the eggs. As the eggs start to set, add croutons and cook. When the center is still moist (but not wet) turn omelet out on a dish and fold over. Sprinkle with parsley and serve immediately.

Roasted Garlic

This is considered a delicacy in many countries and makes your home smell like an Italian restaurant for several days after you make it up.

1 cup olive oil
8 whole garlic bulbs (not cloves)
1 teaspoon salt
¼ teaspoon pepper
1 large round loaf of dark pumpernickel,
    torn in pieces

Use 1 tablespoon of olive oil to grease the bottom of an 8-inch baking pan. Make a shallow incision all around each garlic head, halfway between the top and bottom, cutting through the papery skin but not into the meat of the garlic cloves. Lift off the pointed top of each head.

Arrange the heads in a pan. Pour remaining olive oil over the garlic heads. Sprinkle with salt and pepper. Bake, uncovered, at 200 degrees for 15 minutes. Cover whole pan with foil and bake 1 to 1½ hours, or until the garlic is tender.

Now comes the fun part. Break apart the head, remove a clove, and squeeze the contents onto a piece of bread while the clove is still warm.

Aioli (Garlic Mayonnaise)

Why use regular mayo on a sandwich or in chicken salad when you can have aioli?

1 egg yolk
1 cup olive oil
1 tablespoon wine vinegar
  Salt and pepper to taste
4 cloves garlic, crushed or pounded

Beat egg yolk for 1 minute, then start adding oil, drop by drop, beating continuously. A food processor works well if you have one: pour the oil in while the machine is beating. When over half the oil has been added, the mixture should start to thicken. Stop adding oil and begin to beat in the vinegar. Begin adding oil again, drop by drop, until the mixture begins to thicken again. If it won't thicken or begins to curdle, break a fresh egg yolk into a clean bowl and slowly beat this into the mixture. Crush or pound garlic, add salt and pepper to taste, and mix in.

Note: Whenever you are working with raw eggs, be very careful that your ingredients are not left exposed at room temperature for long periods of time. Keep your aioli refrigerated when you are not using it, and make sure you put it back in the cold after serving it. If you are concerned about using eggs, or have a condition that precludes eating eggs, make your aioli with pasterized egg yolks, available in the frozen section of your grocery store.

REMEDIES

Garlic has been called "heal-all," and you can see how appropriate that name is if you consider the range of maladies it can ease. Garlic has antibiotic qualities, attacking bacteria much like penicillin. Whether its strong smell repels bacteria or it actually does kill bacteria remains a mystery.

Hippocrates, the fifth-century B.C. Greek doctor who is known as the father of modern medicine, was the first Western medical practitioner who believed that medicine was a science not a religion: among his many cures, he used garlic for infections, wounds, cancer, leprosy, digestive disorders, and ailments of the heart. In the first century A.D., the Roman naturalist, Pliny the Elder, recommended garlic for colds, epilepsy, and tapeworm. The sixteenth-century medical innovator Culpepper used garlic when treating all diseases.

Garlic prevents blood clots by making the blood less "sticky" so it will not stick together. It opens blood vessels to reduce blood pressure. This quality was applied in medieval India, where garlic was used to wash wounds and external ulcers. During World War I, Army doctors soaked sphagnum moss in garlic juice and applied it to infected wounds; this treatment was also used to guard against gangrene. It was used for typhus in the same period, and the results proved better than when using penicillin.

Garlic contains vitamin C, which prevents scurvy, and it has traditionally been used to fight tuberculosis, and to eliminate lead and other toxic metals from the body. Garlic is effective against bacteria resistant to antibiotics and will only destroy the bacteria, leaving the body's natural flora unharmed. And, to top off all these positive qualities, garlic contains potassium and is rich in sulfur.

The Native Americans provide our best example of the positive uses of garlic as a healing plant: they would eat garlic to guard against scurvy, as well as combatting the diseases Europeans brought, such as smallpox, which the native peoples had never encountered. Garlic was also fed to cattle by early American pioneers to prevent anthrax.

Fresh garlic can be used to make infusions, tinctures, and other preparations, but in some cases capsules are more desirable since the garlic is not released until the capsule dissolves, thus preventing the problem of breath odor. In the old days, garlic was placed inside of shoes, with the belief that its beneficial properties would be transferred through the skin into a person's body.

Refer to chapter 1 for information about preparing garlic in infusions, etc., and please see the medical disclaimer in the introduction of this book.

Here are two recipes for garlic syrup that should keep any illness far, far away. They can be taken for general health, 1 teaspoonful every morning. Be careful, because you will smell of garlic.

Garlic Syrup I

Peel 3 entire bulbs (heads). Simmer in a non-aluminum pan with 2 cups water. When cloves are soft and there is about 1 cup water left in the pan, remove the garlic and place in a sealable jar. Add to the pan 1 cup cider vinegar and ¼ cup honey. Boil until this mixture gets syrupy. Pour over garlic in the jar and cover to stand over night. The reason a non-aluminum pan is used in this recipe is that aluminum has a tendency to change the chemical compound of vinegar, rendering it ineffective (i.e., not as acidic). Always use non-aluminum pans, containers, and stoppers in bottles when using vinegar.

Garlic Syrup II

Slice one pound of garlic into 1 quart of water. Bruise 1 ounce caraway, 1 ounce fennel seed, and add to the garlic water. Boil until garlic is soft. Let stand 12 to 14 hours in a covered container. Measure at the end of 14 hours and add an equal amount of cider vinegar to whatever measurement you have.

Example: If you have 2½ cups of garlic water, you add 2½ cups vinegar. Bring this mixture to a boil and add enough sugar to make a syrup.

The following are general remedies. For the multiple remedies, try one, and if it doesn't work or you don't like the effects it produces, try another. The only warning I can give you is: chew parsley after taking garlic, if you value your family and friends.

Colds —Take one clove of garlic, chopped and mixed with mayonnaise, on a slice of bread at night at the first sign of a sore throat and runny nose. The cold will be gone by morning.

—A Russian remedy advises to keep a clove of garlic in the mouth between the cheek and teeth. Do not chew. Occasionally release juice by digging the teeth into the clove. Replace garlic clove every 3 to 4 hours. The cold should be gone in about 24 hours.

—Combine 1 crushed clove of garlic, ½ teaspoon cayenne, the juice of 1 lemon, and 1 teaspoon honey. Take this along with vitamin C, 3 times a day at mealtime.

—Peel and crush six cloves of garlic. Mix into ¾ cup white lard or vegetable shortening. Spread this mixture on the soles of the feet and cover with a warm towel. Put paper towels under the feet to absorb grease. Apply fresh every 5 hours until the cold is gone.

—Eat a clove of garlic or take the juice 3 times a day to deter the symptoms of a cold.

Sinus —Crush one clove into ¼ cup water. Draw liquid into eyedropper. Squirt 8 drops of the clear garlic water (strain garlic pieces out) into each nostril, 3 times a day for 3 days. By the third day the infection should clear.

—Take 2 garlic pills and 2 parsley pills every 4 waking hours. After 6 days the infection should clear.

—Eat 2 garlic cloves 3 times a day for 1 week and the infection will clear.

—At first sign of infection, take raw garlic in honey every 2 to 3 hours. This can be mixed with licorice, either juice from the plant or in candy form. This remedy can be taken for colds, fevers, and sinus infections.

Cough—To ease a cough, combine 1 quart boiling water, 1 pound fresh sliced garlic and steep for 12 hours. Add enough sugar to produce a syrupy consistency. Add honey and take 4 times a day.

Sore Throat—Make an infusion by chopping several cloves of garlic and steep in ½ cup water for 6 to 8 hours. Gargle with the infusion to ease the sore throat.

Fever—Bind peeled cloves to the bottom of the feet to stop a fever.

Diarrhea—Add 1 teaspoon of finely chopped garlic to 1 teaspoon honey and take 3 times a day, 2 hours after each meal, until diarrhea stops.

Earache—Puncture 1 garlic oil capsule and squeeze the contents into the ear. Plug with cotton. There should be relief in just half an hour.

Colitis —Take 1 garlic capsule once a week to prevent colitis.

Headache—Mix 1 teaspoon honey in ½ teaspoon garlic juice and swallow. The headache should be gone in about half an hour.

Tinnitus (ringing in the ears)—Put 6 cloves of garlic in the blender and add 1 cup olive oil. Blend until the garlic is minced. Spoon into a glass jar and allow to steep, covered, for 1 week. Strain and apply several drops in the ear daily until ringing stops.

Blood Pressure —Make a special tincture by soaking ½ pound peeled garlic cloves in 1 quart brandy. Shake a few times each day for 2 weeks, then strain. Keeps for about a year and it is safe to take 25 drops per day.

—Eat a clove of garlic 6 times a day. After 4 weeks, blood pressure will drop.

—Eat raw garlic every day in salads, or use in cooking blood pressure friendly foods.

—Take 4 garlic capsules a day, 2 after breakfast and 2 after dinner.

Asthma—Take 1 or 2 cloves with a spoonful of garlic syrup every morning on an empty stomach to prevent asthma.

Arthritis—Rub a clove of garlic on the painful area and take 2 garlic capsules after breakfast, repeating after dinner. The pain of arthritis should be relieved in 24 hours.

Indigestion—To prevent indigestion, take 2 garlic capsules after lunch, and again after dinner. This helps stimulate the secretion of digestive enzymes, thus stopping indigestion.

Boils—Make a poultice of cooked, minced garlic and apply to the boil to draw out the infection.

Insomnia—Rub soles of the feet and nape of the neck with peeled garlic cloves. This should put you right to sleep.

Epilepsy—To reduce seizures caused by epilepsy, make an infusion and take a few tablespoons before and after every meal.

Rheumatism—Pound a clove of garlic with honey and take for 2 or 3 nights successively. This should stop the pain in a few days.

Food Poisoning—Take an infusion of garlic with lemon juice every two hours until symptoms of food poisoning stop.

Toothache—Place one peeled clove of garlic on the affected tooth and keep it there for 1 hour. When you go to the dentist (and you should as soon as you can) please remember to explain this remedy before you open your mouth.

Diverticulitis—Take 1 garlic capsule 3 times a day. This counteracts the bacteria that gets trapped in the diverticuli.

Burns—Puncture a garlic oil capsule and squeeze contents onto the burn. Remember, serious burns should be treated by a physician immediately.

Smelling Salts—Use crushed garlic under the nose to bring the victim back to consciousness.

Appetite Suppressant—Rub a clove of garlic on the upper lip before eating to suppress the appetite.

Athlete's Foot—Apply 1 clove crushed garlic to the affected area and leave on for 1 hour. Wash with water. Do this once a day. If extreme burning, occurs wash immediately, wait and try again with diluted juice.

COSMETIC USES

I don't think it is any surprise that there aren't many cosmetic uses for garlic. Here are the very few I am aware of.

Acne—Mix the juice of 2 garlic cloves with equal amounts vinegar. Dab on pimples every evening.

Hair Loss —An hour before bed, slice open a clove of garlic and rub on the hairless area. Then, right before you go to bed, massage the spot with olive oil, put on a shower cap, and go to bed. Shampoo out in the morning. Repeat for 2 or 3 weeks.

—Macerate 3 to 4 bulbs in 1 quart of wine. Apply to bald area at night and wash out in the morning.

AROMATIC USES

You must be kidding!

OTHER USES

Garlic can be used for many garden purposes. The best method of application is to decant an infusion in a garden spray bottle and apply as necessary.

Pest Control—Garlic can be used to control aphids by making an infusion of 2 crushed cloves of garlic for each 2½ cups water. Red spiders can be controlled by using the same infusion, and deer can be frightened away as well. Japanese Beetles can be controlled by planting garlic around the edge of a garden. They control mosquitoes in California by spraying breeding ponds with garlic and oil, which kills the larvae.

Plant Diseases—A garlic infusion can control potato blight. Black spot can be stopped with an infusion as well.

Companion Planting—Plant garlic with cabbage, eggplant, tomatoes, and roses. Garlic contains natural fungicides. Plant under peach trees to control leaf curl. Do not plant near beans and peas, as their growth will be inhibited by the dominant nature of garlic.

8

LEMON BALM, STEPCHILD OF THE LEMON

Lemon balm is a perennial, so it will return year after year (and you'll be glad for it). With scalloped green to gold leaves, lemon balm looks a great deal like mint, with good reason, since it is part of the mint family. One way to tell the difference is to crush a leaf and test the scent given off: lemon balm will smell of lemon, while mint smells minty. It grows two to three feet in height and blooms with white, yellowish, or pink flowers from July through September.

HISTORY, MAGIC, AND FOLKLORE

The ancient Greeks knew of lemon balm, if we are to judge by its mention in Homer's *Odyssey*, an epic poem at least 2,700 years old. Pliny the Elder, the Roman naturalist writing in the middle of the first century, suggests attaching a sprig of balm to a sword when going into battle since it would staunch any wounds received. Shakespeare also makes reference to the plant in several of his plays. In the Victorian language of flowers it signifies sympathy.

Other names for lemon balm are Balm and Melissa (its botanical name is *Melissa officianalis*).

The herb has been used to treat both scorpion and dog bites, and is known as an attractor of bees. Why bees? Supposedly, they love lemon balm more than any, as reflected in the tradition that bees will never abandon their hive if lemon balm is growing nearby. This has given rise to the practice of many beekeepers of rubbing the inside of a new hive with lemon balm in order to attract a swarm of bees.

Magically, lemon balm has the power to bring people together, and so can be employed in enchantments for love, prosperity, or success. A sachet can be carried or given to someone with whom you wish to have a relationship. Perhaps with a nod to the bees, inhaling the scent is said to encourage attraction between two people. Lemon balm can be burned as incense to attract a lover or to evoke success and prosperity. Bathing in water infused with lemon balm is said to give the bather prosperity, and a byproduct of the process is that one's skin will benefit from lemon balm's soothing qualities. Include lemon balm in dream pillows to encourage prophetic dreams.

PROPAGATION AND CULTIVATION

Lemon balm isn't picky. It tolerates any soil, and will grow in full or partial sun, or in the shade. This is one of the few herbs whose seeds are easy to grow. There are no special requirements: just sow the seed in the ground in early spring or late fall. Lemon balm is a slow germinator (takes about 2 to 3 weeks), though it will germinate faster if the seeds aren't covered; however, this method is only recommended for indoor germination, since the seeds left uncovered in your garden will blow away or become lunch for the birds.

Plant the seeds in a plastic pop bottle bottom and press down lightly. Make sure the seeds don't dry out. Water and place plastic over the planter, spraying with water every time it looks like the seeds are drying out.

Lemon balm can also be propagated by plant division in the spring, or with cuttings in the spring or summer. Layering is another good method to propagate the plant. Start the layering process in the spring as soon as the branches are long enough and you will have a new plant by August, ready to be planted. If you are lucky (and you probably will be), another plant will begin close to the mother plant all by itself in the spring. This smaller plant can be transplanted as soon as the ground is thawed enough to be dug, and when the danger of frost is past.

This herb is susceptible to powdery mildew. In the first year the plant may be small and a bit scrawny, but give it a year and it will bush out nicely. Clip flowers and tops to encourage bushiness.

HARVEST

Cut lemon balm frequently. Bring the cuttings inside, wash and dry the leaves. Cut the entire plant 2 inches above the ground during the first few weeks of July. Be careful you don't bruise the leaves. Another harvest of about 3 inches above the ground can be taken in late August.

STORAGE

Fresh is best when it comes to lemon balm, but you can freeze it for use in some preparations. Balm can be dried but the oils tend to dissipate quickly and are lost.

CULINARY USES

Lemon balm gives a wonderful lemon flavor to almost anything. If you love lemon, you simply must grow this herb in your garden.

Keep in mind these pointers when cooking with this herb:

Lemon balm is best when used fresh.

Lemon balm makes a lovely tea. Add a little honey to it before drinking.

Toss lemon balm leaves in green salads.

Lemon balm leaves are also tasty in fruit salads.

Add chopped leaves to orange marmalade for a treat.

Here are a few recipes to try.

Lemon Balm Appetizers

Add a fresh taste to your festivities.

> 1 cup flaked chicken (canned or fresh)
> ½ cup mayonnaise
> 1 small cucumber, diced
> 2 tablespoons minced lemon balm
>   Whole, fresh lemon balm leaves

Mix all ingredients but the whole leaves and chill. Spread on crackers or toast rounds, then garnish with fresh leaves.

Lemon Balm Pesto

Talk about mouth watering! This is great over broiled or grilled fish.

2 cups fresh lemon balm leaves
2 cloves garlic
½ cup olive oil

Chop lemon balm and garlic finely, then add olive oil. Mix well.

Lemon Balm Jelly

This is great served with fish and poultry.

Box of powdered pectin
Yellow food coloring
Leaves of lemon balm

Make recipe for apple jelly per directions on box of pectin. After skimming the foam from the boiling jelly, add 2 drops yellow food coloring. Place 3 leaves of lemon balm in each jelly jar and pour jelly over. Seal. This should make 3 or 4 jars.

Melissa Punch

A great thirst quencher during the summer, I like this best with sparkling apple cider—but ginger ale works just fine.

2 quarts water
2 handfuls lemon balm leaves
4 sprigs lemon verbena or lemon grass
Ginger ale or sparkling apple cider

Bring water to a boil and place the herbs in the pan. Simmer for 10 minutes. Steep until cold. Strain. Measure this mixture and place in a punch bowl. Add an equal amount of ginger ale or sparkling cider. Serve with ice. Float lemon balm leaves on the surface, or make an ice ring with lemon balm leaves frozen inside.

Fresh "Balmed" Fruit

Summer salads will never taste as good without the fresh lemon flavor of balm.

> 1 small watermelon
> 1 large cantaloupe
> 1 honeydew melon
> ½ pound Bing cherries
> ½ pound green seedless grapes
> 1 tablespoon lemon balm leaves
> 3 tablespoons fresh mint leaves
> 1 pound peaches (fresh only)
> 1 cup sherry

Cut watermelon lengthwise in half and scoop out pulp with a melon baller. Do the same with the cantaloupe and honeydew. Pit and cut cherries in half. Remove grapes from their stems. Slice peaches. Place all in a large bowl and add mint and balm leaves. Marinate for at least 12 to 24 hours with the sherry. Return the fruit mixture to the watermelon shell and decorate with sprigs of balm and mint.

Note: Add peaches last to keep them from browning. Once the peach slices are covered with sherry they won't brown.

Lemon Balm Butter

Perhaps an unusual taste for most, but it will be accepted after the first bite!

> 1 stick butter
> 2 tablespoons chopped lemon balm
> ½ teaspoon honey

Combine well and serve over hot vegetables or lamb.

Balm Lemonade

This lemonade tastes a bit different from the regular kind, and is much better than the stuff you make from powder—a real treat!

4 lemons
Bunch of lemon balm
½ cup sugar
⅔ cup boiled water
2½ cups cold water
Sprigs of lemon balm

Scrub lemons and peel rinds thinly. Place rinds in a heat-proof pitcher. Tear the balm into ¼-inch pieces and add to the rind along with the sugar. Pour boiling water over and stir. Infuse for 15 minutes. Cut lemons in half and squeeze juice out into another container. Strain seeds out. Place sprigs into a serving pitcher and pour in lemon juice. Add cooled syrup mixture and cold water. Chill. Place sprigs in the lemonade.

REMEDIES

Refer to chapter 1 for information about preparing lemon balm in infusions, etc., and please see the medical disclaimer in the introduction of this book. Please do not use these remedies if you are pregnant, as the herb will induce menstruation. Also, don't use these if you have a thyroid condition, especially if you are taking thyroid medication (lemon balm inhibits thyroid hormones).

Headache—An infusion will ease a headache. Take one cup and relax for a while.

Nausea—Take 1 cup infusion, unsweetened, to quell nausea.

Toothache—Drink 1 cup infusion and put drops of peppermint oil on the tooth. This will stop the toothache until you can get to a dentist.

Digestion —Take 1 cup infusion after meals to aid in digestion.

Flatulence—Take a strong infusion after meals to inhibit the effects of flatulence (lemon balm is an antispasmodic).

Eczema—To ease the itch and scale of eczema, use the oil to massage into the affected area.

Menstruation—An infusion will promote bleeding.

Fever—An infusion induces sweating, thus easing the fever.

Mumps—Use oil on mumps. Rub into affected area to relieve pain.

Cold Sores—Use oil on cold sores. Lemon balm is an antiviral and will prevent sores from getting worse.

Depression—A seventeenth-century remedy calls for lemon balm steeped in wine and drunk nightly: "Comforts the heart and driveth away melancholy and sadness" (John Evelyn).

Sedative—Take 1 cup strong infusion before bed to send you to sleep safely and quickly.

Stomach Cramps—Take 1 cup strong infusion to stop stomach cramps.

Anxiety—Take a strong infusion to relieve nervous anxiety.

Bleeding—Bruise balm and apply leaves to wound, binding with a bandage (remember Pliny the Elder's trick of tying the herb on a warrior's sword). Leave on until the bleeding stops.

COSMETIC USES

Lemon balm cleanses and relaxes the skin. Use a strong infusion on acne. Dab it on the affected area and let air-dry. You can use a regular infusion to cleanse each night, as it is quite gentle. An infusion applied every morning will soothe wrinkles.

AROMATIC USES

Place a handful of lemon balm and about ½ cup oatmeal in a muslin bath bag. You can make a bath bag in two different ways.

—Cut a 6-inch by 6-inch square of muslin, place the herb in the center and bring all corners up tying with either a rubber band or string.

—Or you can cut a 6 by 13-inch rectangle. Bring the edges together to make a 6-inch square and sew around the two side edges (A). The fold will create the bottom. Fold down the top of the bag about half an inch and sew at the bottom of the seam, leaving a ½-inch opening in which to insert ribbon (B). Cut about 1 yard of ¼-inch satin ribbon, knot one end, and place a safety pin in the other. Fish this through the casting you made at the top of your bag (C). Bring ribbon up to be equal on both sides pulling pleats into the muslin bag, and tie it at the top so that it can be hung from the faucets in the tub (D).

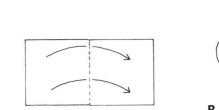

A

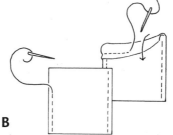

B

C

D

Throw your full bath bag into the bath water and let steep for about 5 minutes. Hop in and rub on skin. The lemon balm will cleanse, the oatmeal will soften the skin, and the scent will wipe away any trace of depression.

To keep your bath bag clean, try putting your lemon balm in a paper coffee filter, gathering the edges, and tying it off with a rubber band. Tuck this little packet into the bath bag and proceed to take your bath. This will prevent a messy cleanup after your bath: just throw the used coffee filter away.

Lemon balm can be used for potpourri as well.

Lemony Fresh Potpourri

A great, natural air freshener and aromatic pick-me-up.

        1 cup lemon balm leaves, dried
        ½ cup lemon verbena leaves, dried
        ½ cup lemon grass, dried and chopped
        1 cup lemon geranium leaves
        2 tablespoons dried lemon rind
           Several dehydrated lemon
           wedges or rounds
        ½ cup orris root
        2–4 drops lemon verbena or lemon balm oil
           (essential oils)

Combine and place in open jar in kitchen. It will give off a lovely lemon scent.

ORNAMENTAL USES

Lemon balm lends a nice touch to the landscape. In the sun the leaves will be bright green, while in the shade they tend to be a little more golden green.

OTHER USES

Lemon balm can be used as an insect repellent. Rub a leaf on the kitchen table to keep ants and bugs away. When camping or celebrating out of doors, throw it into the camp- or bonfire to deter mosquitoes.

Lemon balm can be used as furniture polish, as William Shakespeare explains in *The Merry Wives of Windsor.* Just rub a few leaves on wood and the oil that is deposited works like a polish.

9

MINT, THE HOSPITABLE COMPANION

Mint is one of the easiest herbs to grow. Actually, a better way to put it is, mint is probably the hardest herb to get rid of. My grandmother grew it, as did my mother, and I am keeping the family tradition alive, along with everyone else I know. Most people "underuse" this herb, not realizing its potential beyond being a garnish.

Mint is a perennial that will return year after year after year, ad infinitem. Most varieties have squarish stems that grow 2 to 3 feet, and they flower in July and August. All

mint plants have toothed or scalloped leaves, with blooms growing on stalks and mostly hairy leaves and stems. Mint is a native of Europe and Asia, but has been naturalized throughout North America.

Here are just a few of the many varieties of mint.

TYPES OF MINT

Apple Mint—Sometimes referred to as woolly mint, despite the fact that woolly mint is a different variety altogether. Apple mint has a flavor akin to the fruit, gray-green leaves covered with down, and purple flowers. It grows 2 to 3 feet high.

Orange Mint—Also known as bergamot mint, its lemon-orange scent provides its name. This variety has smooth, grass-green leaves accented with reddish purple stems and a lavender flower. This variety has been used as an herbal room deodorizer.

Black Peppermint—This mint has forest-green leaves with deep purple veins and stems and purple flowers. Its scent is very strong and can be used in culinary dishes, but it is better used as an aromatic or remedy herb.

Peppermint—Sometimes called white peppermint, this variety is grass-green with reddish purple undertones and violet flowers. It is good for freshening the air, keeping harmful insects away from cabbage, and when used in tea or potpourri.

Spearmint—This is probably the most common type of mint, also known as lamb mint, pea mint, or garden mint. It has textured, light green leaves and violet-gray flowers. It grows to about 30 inches tall. Spearmint does well in jellies, teas, and fruit salads. The variety is also know for its use in repelling flies.

Pineapple Mint—This mint has a wonderful pineapple scent (surprise) with creamy, off-white colored splotches amid apple-green leaves. It adds a fresh flavor to fruit salads.

Ginger Mint—This mint is purely ornamental with greenish yellow leaves, and grows about 15 inches tall.

Curly Mint —Curly mint has ruffled green leaves with white or lilac flowers. It grows to 2½ feet high.

Corsican Mint—Some say this variety possesses the "true mint" flavor. It has small mossy leaves, is fairly tender (which means it won't survive a snowy winter in northern climes), and needs partial shade: no full sun for this mint. It only grows to about 1 inch high. This is the variety used to make crème de menthe.

Pennyroyal —Pennyroyal creeps along in a matted growth. It has a strong scent and sports small green leaves with violet-blue flowers. This variety is for aromatic use only, and serves well as a ground cover. Use this variety when trying to get rid of fleas and moths. It can grow to almost 3 inches. Make sure you know which kind of mint you are about to eat: if it's pennyroyal, you'd better put it down and walk away, since it can be quite toxic if ingested.

HISTORY, MAGIC, AND FOLKLORE

There is a legend in Greek mythology concerning the origin of mint. Persephone, the wife of the Hades, king of the underworld, found out that her mate was in love with a beautiful nymph named Menthe. She became jealous and changed the nymph into a plant. Over time, her name changed to Minthe, then to Mint.

Another story from ancient Greece concerns two strangers who travelled throughout Asia Minor. They were ignored by the villagers in every town they entered and were offered neither food nor drink. One day Philemon and Baucis, an elderly couple, offered them a meal as the two passed by the couple's farm. Before setting the table they rubbed it with mint leaves to make sure it was clean and fresh for their guests. Then, as the strangers sat down at the table, they revealed themselves as Zeus and Hermes, gods in disguise who had set out to test mankind. Philemon and Baucis were awarded for their hospitality: the gods changed their humble home into a temple. Since that time, mint has been the symbol of hospitality.

In fact, the great civilizations of the ancient Mediterranean knew mint quite well: Greeks made a practice of using it in their temple rites, while the later Romans would crown themselves with peppermint wreaths. Apicius, the author of a Roman cookbook published around A.D. 37, gives recipes using mint. Mint grows wild in Israel, and in the Gospel of Matthew Jesus rails against the Pharisees for demanding tithes to be paid in mint.

Later, when Western civilization got a little less civilized, mint was used as a strewing herb during the Middle Ages. Shakespeare mentions mint in *A Winter's Tale* and *Love's Labour's Lost*. It is said that mint can produce wisdom by inhaling its scent, and in the Victorian language of flowers mint means virtue.

The most common of mint's varieties are peppermint and spearmint, both of which grow abundantly in many neighborhood yards and gardens, even growing wild in some places. Both types of mint are similar in their magical uses, but there are a few differences. Spearmint's folknames are Gardenmint, Green Spine, Spiremint, Our Lady's mint, Mackeral mint, and Brown mint. Peppermint is also called Lammint and Brandymint.

Both spearmint and peppermint can be included in love sachets or incense. Peppermint is used as a protection herb, and a sachet of it should be carried for protection when traveling. Many people wash down their floors and walls with a diluted infusion of mint in order to exorcise negative energy. A sachet can be sniffed periodically when taking written examinations to keep the brain clear and alert for the test. The fragrance of mint also helps writers: I have bowls of it in my writing area. It is also believed that mint will attract prosperity, so make sure you keep a sprig in your wallet or purse. Peppermint has also been used in certain contexts to stimulate passion.

Place mint in mixtures for dream pillows. Its pleasant scent will bring on clairvoyant dreams and will protect the sleeper from nightmares.

PROPAGATION AND CULTIVATION

Since mint is a perennial, it prefers moist soil and shade, but will tolerate sun to a degree. Just make sure you don't put it where the sun will beat down on it 12 hours a day. At night, mint will survive night temperatures down to the 40s; if the temperature dips lower, your mint will need a little protection.

Keep different mint varieties separated, placing them far apart from each other. Your spearmint can go on one side of the house, your peppermint on the other side, orange mint around back, and maybe your apple mint can go in a small patch next to the garage. If mint plants are placed near each other, their individual flavors will be weakened through cross-pollination (since bees don't know the difference between mint varieties, and they don't care).

Mint is a sterile hybrid, which means it doesn't produce seed. The only way mint can be propagated is through cuttings, division, and layering. Cuttings can be started in the spring. Division can be done after all danger of frost is past and your plant produces a few leaves. You can also divide in the early fall. Layering should be done in the spring, then transplant the young plant in late August.

Mint can be planted in containers, but they must be big ones, about 12 inches deep. I have a friend who planted mint in a whiskey barrel and she says it is trying to break out and free itself to the wild, so even in a container mint must be contained. Mint also does well in rock gardens, but I would use the low growing mints such as pennyroyal or Corsican for this.

Mint can be grown indoors as long as there is enough light; if not, it tends to get a bit leggy and straggly. Just remember to divide and re-pot every year, good advice to people like my friend with the whiskey barrel.

Another thing to watch out for with mint is the spread of runners. These are little roots that grow under the ground and surface a few inches, a few feet, even a few yards away from the mother in order to produce more plants. If it's planted in the garden, mint's runners must be contained or they will grow wild. Containing runners is some work, but it's well worth it if you don't want a yard full of mint run amuck.

There are several different methods of containment besides planting in a whiskey barrel, a strategy that obviously didn't work too well. One way is to sink metal barriers 10 inches deep in a square or circle, then plant the mint inside the barrier. Another way is to take 6-inch long ceramic tiles, sink them into the ground so that only 2 or 3 inches are above ground in a circle, and plant your mint inside this. Some people have tried to sink large tin cans without bottoms in the ground and plant their mint inside of these; that probably isn't a good idea since the tin will eventually rust and disintegrate, leaving your mint a chance to escape. I buy cheap plastic buckets or get large pickle buckets (you can get these from restaurants) and cut out the bottoms. I sink them into the ground so that about 3 inches is sticking out and plant my mint inside. If you use buckets, make sure you use new ones since the old ones that you would use to scrub the floor will probably have chemical residues you don't want going into your garden.

Cut your mint after the first of June: this will encourage the plant to branch out over the growing season. In the fall, after your last harvest and before the first frost, cut the whole plant to the ground and mulch. It is recommended that you move your mint to fresh soil every 4 or 5 years, but my mint has been growing in the same place for twice that long and I haven't had any problems. Be careful with peppermint, however, because it tends to strip the soil of all its

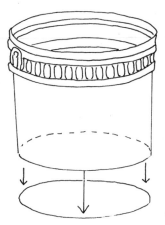

beneficial properties. If you don't want to move it, you should probably add some heavy-duty fertilizer at least once a year. Chicken droppings work best in this capacity. Some people add fire ash to their gardens as fertilizer, which does do some good for other plants but not for this herb: fire ash can be fatal to mint.

Peppermint loves to be planted near broccoli, chamomile, tomatoes, and cabbage. It keeps cabbage moths and other insects away while it encourages the growth of strawberries. Pineapple, apple, or orange mint will benefit both itself and English walnut trees it is planted under.

All mints are susceptible to rust. Make sure your plants are at least 6 inches apart from each other to prevent disease from spreading. Pests include spider mites, beetles, root borers, grasshoppers, cutworms, and aphids. To get rid of these pests, pour soapy water over the affected plants.

HARVEST

You can cut mint at any time. Cut low right before the first frost to get the most harvest you can.

STORAGE

Mint can be dried by hanging in small bunches in a dry area out of sunlight. It also does well in a dehydrator with a screen, while drying mint in the oven or in a microwave expels the essential oils too fast and doesn't work very well. Store your dried mint in airtight containers.

Mint can also be frozen, but it becomes limp and slimy when defrosted.

Culinary Uses

You should try mint jelly if you haven't already. Mint also makes up the main ingredient in that legendary Southern drink, mint julep. When using peppermint only use young leaves, since older leaves tend to be bitter.

Combine plain yogurt, cucumber, and any variety of mint for a cooling salad (known in Greek cooking as "*tzatziki*").

Add mint to tuna or chicken salad for a different taste temptation.

Here are some common, and not so common, recipes using mint.

Mint Sauce

Lamb or beef take on a special flavor when cooked with this sauce.

2 tablespoons water
1 tablespoon sugar
½ cup cider vinegar
½ cup fresh mint leaves, chopped

Heat water and sugar until sugar dissolves. Add the vinegar and chopped leaves and stir until it thickens a bit. Serve over lamb or roast beef.

Mint Sugar

Mint sugar adds flavor to iced tea and fruits, also lends a cooling effect to foods served in the summer heat.

4–6 mint leaves
1 cup sugar

Blend on high in blender. Dry on cookie sheet overnight and place in a jar. Use on cookies, grapefruit, in tea, or roll grapes in it.

Mint Butter

Melt this over potatoes or vegetables (especially peas and beans) for a real treat.

½ pound butter or margarine
2 tablespoons crushed mint
1 tablespoon lemon juice

Combine all ingredients together, either in a food processor or by smashing with a fork until well mixed. Keep refrigerated and serve over hot broiled lamb chops, baked potatoes, or spread on toast and sprinkle with sugar (try with mint sugar—see recipe on page 102).

Mint Jelly

If you've never had mint jelly before, don't be surprised if you don't like it on toast. It is commonly served with lamb in much the same way as cranberry sauce is served with turkey.

6 cups apple juice
½ cup cider vinegar
4 cups fresh mint leaves, crushed
12 cups sugar
2 6-ounce bottles liquid pectin
2 teaspoons mint flavoring
Green food coloring
Sprigs of mint

Boil apple juice, vinegar, and mint leaves for 15 minutes. Stir in sugar and boil. Add pectin and boil 1 minute. Strain. Add favoring and coloring to desired taste and shade. Pour in sterilized jars and add a sprig of mint on top. Seal. This will make about 15 to 20 small jelly jars.

Note: If you are going to seal with paraffin, don't put the sprig on top. It will stick to the lid and make a mess when opened.

Mint Julep

For that antebellum feeling: imagine yourself on the porch of Tara, before the Civil War, sipping this Southern delight while the hot summer wind ruffles your hair. Make sugar syrup a day in advance before serving.

> 1 large handful spearmint leaves
> 2 tablespoons and 2 teaspoons
>   sugar syrup (recipe follows)
> 6 ounces bourbon

Sugar Syrup

> ½ cup water
> ½ cup sugar
> 1 handful mint leaves

Bring water and sugar to a boil and continue to boil until sugar dissolves. Remove from heat. Bruise mint leaves by squishing with the bottom of a heavy drinking glass. This releases the oil. Then add to water/sugar mixture. Cover and refrigerate for 12 to 24 hours. Strain.

Combine 2 tablespoons and 2 teaspoons of sugar syrup (save what you don't use for later) in a pitcher with the bourbon. Stir well and pour in tall glasses filled with cracked ice. Garnish with sprigs of mint.

Make lemonade for the kids with the excess sugar syrup by squeezing about 6 lemons and straining. Add about 1 gallon of water, then add sugar syrup about 2 to 3 tablespoons to your taste. You can add a sprig of mint to your lemonade for a different taste.

Mint Fizzer

The kids will enjoy this drink while you're drinking your julep.

¼ cup chopped mint
1½ tablespoons sugar
⅔ cup boiled water
   Juice of 1 orange or ¼ cup orange juice
   Juice of 1 lemon, fresh-squeezed
1 cup ginger ale or soda water
6 ice cubes
1 sprig mint

Put chopped mint into a heat-proof pitcher with sugar and pour boiled water over top. Cool. Add juices. Chill for 2 to 3 hours and strain. Add ginger ale or soda water and ice. Decorate with a sprig.

Mint Tea

This will wake you up in the morning without the caffeine!

1 teaspoon dried mint leaves
1 cup boiling water
   Honey to taste

Combine 1 teaspoon of dried leaves to 1 cup boiling water. Let stand covered 10 minutes, then add honey.

Mint Iced Tea

Nothing's cooler and more refreshing than this drink.

6–8 sprigs mint
4 cups water

Wash mint and liquefy in the blender with water. Let stand 30 minutes, strain and sweeten.

Note: Add two tea bags while standing for a tea flavored with mint.

Mint Punch

Very cooling drink for an outdoor summer function.

> 2 cups boiling water
> 8 mint teabags
> 1½ cups lemonade
> 2 cups orange juice
> 2 cups crushed ice
> 1 (12-ounce) can of ginger ale

Boil water and place teabags in to steep. Steep until cool. Meanwhile place in a punch bowl lemonade and orange juice. Pour in cooled tea mixture. Add ice and ginger ale. Serve.

Minted Grapefruit

Make this up the night before you plan to serve for breakfast. Watch your family's eyes pop open.

> 2 cans grapefruit sections, drained
>   (save the juice)
> 1 cup sugar
> 2 tablespoons fresh mint

Combine in a pan ½ cup of the grapefruit juice, sugar, and mint. Bring to a boil and keep boiling 5 minutes. Cool. Place fruit in a bowl and add cooled syrup. Mix well and chill.

Mint Nut Bread

A different twist to nut breads that'll please your taste buds.

2½ cups flour
1 cup firmly packed brown sugar
3½ teaspoons baking powder
3 tablespoons vegetable oil
¾ cup apple juice
¾ cup milk
1 egg
1 cup chopped walnuts or pecans
1 cup chopped mint leaves, fresh,
    or ⅓ cup dried (fresh works
    better in this recipe)

Preheat oven to 350 degrees. Mix flour, sugar, and baking powder in a large bowl. In another bowl, whisk together oil, apple juice, milk, and egg. Add to dry ingredients, combining well. Add nuts and mint. Bake in a greased bread pan for 50 to 60 minutes until bread tests done (i.e., insert a toothpick and make sure it comes out clean).

Mint Vinegar

This can be used to make salad dressings and marinades, but is also good for a facial wash.

1 gallon white vinegar
8 cups crushed mint leaves

Place leaves in vinegar and let stand for 1 month. Strain and place in bottles with a fresh sprig.

Tabooleh

This is a Middle Eastern dish with an unusual yet satisfying taste. You may have seen it on restaurant menus spelled "tabouleh" or "tabouli."

        1 cup bulgur (cracked wheat)
        5 tomatoes
        1 bunch green onions
        2 large bunches parsley
        1 cup fresh mint leaves
           Juice of 3 lemons
        ¼ cup olive oil
           Salt and pepper to taste

Rinse wheat bulgur and soak in hot water for 10 minutes. Drain. Clean and chop tomatoes, onions, parsley, and mint. Squeeze water from the wheat and place in a bowl. Add chopped vegetables and herbs. Add lemon juice, oil, and salt and pepper and toss. Serve cold. Serves 6.

Minty Grapefruit Sorbet

A little taste of heaven on a hot summer day!

           Juice from 2 large grapefruits
        ½ cup sugar
        ⅔ cup water
        3 sprigs mint
        1 egg white, or egg white powder
              to equal 1 egg white
           Mint leaves

Squeeze juice from grapefruits and strain. Boil sugar and water in a pan until sugar is dissolved. Put in sprigs, cover and cool 20 minutes. Strain and cool completely. Mix cooled syrup with juice and pour in rigid container (a 9 x 13-inch metal cake pan works well). Freeze until semi-frozen, 45 minutes to 1 hour. Beat egg white until stiff and fold into sorbet. Freeze until firm, about 1 or 2 hours. Serve garnished with mint leaves.

Note: Use powder if you're nervous about this because of possible food poisoning.

Mint Cookies

There are several variants for these yummy cookies. My favorite is to glaze with chocolate. Try these at Christmas.

- 1 cup butter
- ½ cup sugar
- ¼ teaspoon peppermint extract
- 2 tablespoons crushed dried mint
- 2 cups flour
- ¼ teaspoon salt

Cream butter and sugar. Add extract and mix well. In another bowl combine mint, flour, and salt. Add slowly to creamed mixture, mixing well. Chill dough. Form into 1-inch balls, roll in sugar (see the instructions for making mint sugar recipe on page 102), and place on greased cookie sheet. Press with thumb in the middle. Bake at 350 degrees for 12 to 15 minutes. Makes 3 dozen.

Variations: Add chocolate chips or nuts to the cookie. You can ice with a melted chocolate glaze. I use ½ cup semisweet chocolate chips melted in a double boiler with 2 tablespoons shortening. You can also glaze with a mixture of powdered sugar, milk, and green food coloring, then sprinkle with crushed peppermint candy.

Mystic Mynt Myst

This gelatin dessert is guaranteed to cool anyone down.

1 (20½-ounce) can of crushed pineapple
1 (10-ounce) jar of mint jelly (use your own)
1 package lime gelatin
¼ cup chopped walnuts or pecans
1 small container non-dairy whipped topping
1 cup mini-marshmallows (or use more
     if you want)

Drain pineapple and reserve juice. Place juice in a pan with the jelly and heat until jelly dissolves and becomes liquid. Add gelatin. Remove from heat and stir to dissolve. Add pineapple and nuts. Cool in the refrigerator until syrupy or becomes the consistency of an egg white. Fold in non-dairy whipped topping and marshmallows. Freeze until firm. Before serving, let thaw slightly and cut in squares.

Minty Chocolates

Chocolate combined with mint: need I say more?

1 pound chocolate almond bark
1 pound vanilla bark
     (you can get barks at any
     good candy store)
2 cups fresh mint, finely chopped in
     the food processor

Melt barks separately over hot water. Combine mint with chocolate bark. This mixture should be pretty thick. Keep over hot water. Drop small amounts of the chocolate/mint mixture with a buttered spoon into candy papers. As soon as these are firm, top with some of the melted vanilla bark by spooning on with your buttered spoon. Sprinkle with crushed peppermint candy on top, if desired.

REMEDIES

Mint is a very powerful healing herb, which means its benefits are many, but so are its possible dangerous side effects. Never use mint oil in its pure form, always using instead an amount diluted with water: pure mint oil can be toxic if used incorrectly. Be sure never to give mint oil (even diluted) to young children. See also the warning about laryngitis below.

Don't let these warnings put you off using mint as a remedy: with a little common sense, the herb can be unbeatable. For instance, mint in the form of incense provides the perfect atmosphere when working a healing. It is especially beneficial to those with lung diseases or any respiratory ailments. If you rub a sprig of mint on your skin, you will instantly feel its cooling, antibiotic effect; this characteristic can be used in treatments by merely rubbing mint leaves directly on the affected area of a patient's body to ease symptoms. Mint is an antispasmodic (it relaxes muscles) and an antibiotic (it helps eliminate infection).

Refer to chapter 1 for information about preparing mint in infusions, etc., and please see the medical disclaimer in the introduction of this book.

Use peppermint in all remedies unless otherwise indicated.

Indigestion—Take a hot infusion, or heat a cup of milk and add 2 tablespoons mint. Drink to ease an upset stomach.

Stomach Flu—Mix together 2 tablespoons dry peppermint and 2 tablespoons bruised caraway seed. Measure 1 teaspoon into a cup and add boiling water (save the rest in a tin to use later). Steep 15 minutes, covered, then strain and sweeten with honey. This works exceptionally well in stopping the symptoms of stomach flu.

Nausea—Chew mint leaves to ease nausea. Peppermint works best, though spearmint can also be used.

Flatulence—Place 2 or 3 drops peppermint oil on an ice cube and lick. This works exceptionally well.

Heartburn—Take a strong infusion when symptoms of heartburn appear.

Liver—Take an infusion once a day. This stimulates the bile and increases liver function.

Gall Bladder—Take an infusion twice a day. This stimulates the bile and it may move gallstones out of the way if they are stuck in the gall bladder. This treatment may also irritate the situation, so be very careful and see a doctor as soon as possible.

Cold or Flu—Make an infusion, adding chamomile, and sip a cup until symptoms of the cold disappear.

Menstruation—Drink an infusion. Unlike other herbs covered in this book, there are no warnings against pregnant women taking mint. That is because mint does not promote bleeding. Instead, it relaxes the muscles around the uterus to help cramps go away.

Hunger—An infusion will relieve hunger pangs, but this is only a temporary remedy: after a while they will return, worse than before.

Insomnia—Take an infusion of spearmint, peppermint, or orange mint to induce sleep.

Headache—Apply fresh grated leaves to forehead to stop a headache.

Thrush—Combine 1 tablespoon dried mint and 2 teaspoons dried thyme in 1 cup boiled water. Steep for 30 minutes and strain. Wash mouth with this mixture several times a day.

Toothache—Place diluted peppermint or spearmint oil on tooth. Go see your dentist as soon as possible.

Chapped Hands—Wash hands with a spearmint infusion and let air-dry. This should relieve the discomfort within a few days.

Bad Breath—Chew leaves to dispel bad breath.

Bee Stings and Insect Bites—Gently rub crushed leaves on the bite after removing stinger. If any part of your body begins to swell (such as the stung area, your tongue or throat), get to the emergency room and forget about herbal remedies: you may be dangerously allergic.

Footbath—Make two recipes of a strong infusion and soak tired, aching feet in it.

Sore Mouth or Throat—Gargle several times a day with a strong infusion to relieve sore mouth and throat.

Laryngitis—Don't take mint, mentholated drinks, or cough drops when you have laryngitis. Mint and its byproducts will dry out your vocal cords, the absolute opposite of what you need: the larynx should be kept moist with this ailment. The best treatment for laryngitis, then, is to drink lots of lemon water.

COSMETIC USES

Mint is great for the skin. It is an astringent, which means it cleanses the oils from the skin leaving it fresh.

A mint steam will refresh your face, and your spirits. Place 1 cup peppermint leaves in a pot of boiling water. Remove from the stove and place the pot on a heat-proof pad on the table or counter. Take a towel and your head and the pan, making a steam tent. Stay under the towel for at least 10 minutes. This will open your pores and release toxins. When you are finished, pat your face dry with the towel. By the way, this will also clear the sinuses.

Mint facial wash is very refreshing on a hot, humid day. Pour 2 cups white vinegar and 2 cups water into a pan. Bring to a boil and add a handful of mint leaves. Remove from heat and let sit uncovered for 3 days. Strain into a bottle and store in the refrigerator. When you become hot and tired, place a little of the liquid on a cotton ball and wipe face and neck. It will rejuvenate your spirits and make you feel fresh and tingly.

Make a mint facial mask for oily skin by beating together 1 egg white, 2 tablespoons dry skim milk, 3 drops mint extract (the kind you cook with), and 6 drops spirit of camphor (found in old-time pharmacies, health food or herbal supply stores). Apply to the face and let dry. Wash mask off with warm water and rinse with cold.

A hair tonic can be made with mint by combining 3 tablespoons dried mint, 1 cup water, and ½ cup vinegar in a non-aluminum pot. Bring to a boil and simmer 15 minutes. Steep until cool and strain into a bottle. Massage this into the scalp before shampooing. This will also get rid of dandruff.

AROMATIC USES

Take a "tea bath." Place some mint in a coffee filter, tie it off, and throw it into your bath after a hard day at work. You will feel refreshed and ready for whatever the evening will bring. Your skin will feel tingly as well.

Mint is hung from the ceiling in hot countries to freshen the air and lend an air of coolness. It has a long-lasting scent.

Mint can be used to increase concentration. Place 2 drops of peppermint oil (the essential oil, not the kind you cook with) on a cloth handkerchief and inhale. Careful how long you do this, because excessive inhalation of mint can damage the nose's mucous membranes, which in turn may cause pain.

Chocolate Mint Ecstasy

This is a festive potpourri featuring mint.

> 1 cup dried mint leaves
> 1 cup dried chocolate mint geranium leaves
> ¼ cup orris root
> 2–4 drops peppermint oil (the essential oil)
> ⅓ cup broken cinnamon sticks
> ½ cup of cut, light green or greenish-blue ribbon

Mix together leaves, root, and oil, then add cinnamon sticks and ribbon.

ORNAMENTAL USES

Some mints can be used as a ground cover. Pennyroyal and Corsican mint are good for this purpose. Just make sure you plant them in the shade.

OTHER USES

Mint is a great repellent for insect and rodent pests. Plant mint near doors or place in pots on open windows to keep insects out of the house. Crushed mint or growing mint next to shrubs will drive out red ants. Peppermint and pennyroyal deter moths. Place these herbs in closets and drawers. They also deter black flea beetles.

Moth Repellent

Here's a good potpourri to keep in your closets.

½ cup lavender
½ cup pennyroyal
1 cup cedar chips
4 drops pennyroyal oil (essential oil)

Place this mixture in a nylon stocking and hang it in a closet or place in drawers.

Mint also repels mice and rats. Place sprigs in the eaves of the attic or grow along the basement wall.

Mint fights fleas on your pets and in your house. Make a homemade flea collar by soaking a leather pet collar in pennyroyal oil for 24 hours. Do not do this if your pet is pregnant, as it can cause the animal to abort. To remove flea eggs, make a strong infusion and sponge your pet once a week for a month. Mix 1 teaspoon pennyroyal essential oil in 2 ounces water. For a small animal, make half of this recipe. This can be applied once a week. Again, if your pet is pregnant, do not use.

Add 4 tablespoons dried mint to cat litter to keep it smelling fresh. Rabbit cages will also benefit from placing mint leaves underneath cages: this will keep flies away and make it smell better.

If you happen to leave your clothing in the washer overnight, freshen the scent by placing mint in a nylon stocking, tying it off, and throwing it in the dryer with the clothes. Your clothes will come out smelling fresh and clean.

10

OREGANO, JOY OF THE MOUNTAINS

No self-respecting Italian family can function without oregano. Sometimes confused with marjoram, it is actually a completely different herb. Nevertheless, oregano used to be called "wild marjoram" in some parts of the world.

Oregano generally has erect, hairy and square stems that grow 1 to 2 feet high. Does that sound familiar? It should if you've read chapter 9, because oregano is part of the mint family. It flowers from July through September.

TYPES OF OREGANO

Dwarf Oregano—This creeping, low-growing plant doesn't grow more than 1 or 2 inches high. It isn't used for cooking, but is merely an ornamental plant.

Pot Marjoram —This variety has a sharp flavor, with white flowers and 2-foot-high stalks of hairy leaves.

Golden Oregano—The golden variety has striking yellow leaves. It is purely ornamental and looks great in the garden.

Greek Oregano—Greek oregano has the strongest flavor of all.

Dittany of Crete—This variety had small woolly leaves and pink to white flowers growing up to 9 inches high in the shade. Dittany is different in that it's an annual. Also, it tastes more like marjoram than other kinds of oregano. This variety is an ingredient of the flavored wine vermouth.

Common Oregano or Wild Marjoram—The most common type of oregano, it's the variety everyone probably has in their gardens. It has round green leaves, grows to about 2 feet high and has white to purple flowers.

HISTORY, MAGIC, AND FOLKLORE

Oregano grows as a native in Asia, Europe, and North Africa. The folk etymology for its name means "joy of the mountain," from the ancient Greeks who used it

internally and externally as a remedy for poisons and convulsions. Conversely, if the plant grew on a person's grave, it was said that the departed was unhappy. In ancient Greece and Rome young couples were crowned with wreaths made of the herb.

Oregano was brought to America by GIs returning from Italy and Greece after World War II. It is after this time that the herb, as a spice, became widely popular in the States on pizza and in sauces.

PROPAGATION AND CULTIVATION

Oregano is a perennial, so it comes back year after year. Buy plants from a nursery in the spring and plant as soon as the danger of frost is past. They will spread, but are easy to contain. You can also propagate by root division in the spring. The herb's seeds are quite tiny, so if you want to start seeds, do it indoors. Sprinkle seeds over a planting medium and leave them alone. Do not cover with soil or press down. Mist with water and cover with plastic. Make sure the temperature under the pot is kept at 70. If the seeds do not germinate in 4 to 5 days, try again.

Oregano prefers to be on the dry side, so it's a good plant to grow in drought conditions. It prefers daytime temperatures about 70 degrees, at night about 60. Prune your oregano as needed. By midsummer, cut it back by half and you will be able to get another harvest in September before winter sets in. Plants are productive for about 1 to 2 years, or longer. Mine has been in the garden for 8 years and is still going strong.

Oregano does well in containers and can be brought into the house in the winter: in fact, it can be grown in the house all year round.

When planting oregano in the garden, plant it near beans: this will enhance their growth and flavor. You can also grow it next to broccoli to repel damaging insects.

Oregano will succumb to root rot and fungal disease. To prevent root rot, make sure your plants drain well. They shouldn't be planted in a low-lying area where water can stand. If your oregano is in a container, it should have drain holes in the bottom; it's also a good idea to put some gravel in the bottom of the pot before

planting. To prevent fungal disease, make sure that air can flow around the plants easily. Placing plants up against a building or crowding them with many other plants can encourage this sort of ailment.

Pests who like to make trouble for oregano include spider mites, aphids, or leaf miners. Combat these bugs by pouring soapy water over the affected plants.

Harvest

Oregano can be harvested whenever you need some. Sprigs can be snipped when the plant is about 6 inches tall. In June, when the plant is budding, cut the plant down, leaving only the lower set of leaves. It will leaf back out in about 2 weeks. Cut again towards the end of August.

Storage

Oregano can be frozen. Place leaves in ice cube trays full of water, freeze, and then pop the cubes into freezer bags for storage. Use in stews and soups. You can also freeze sprigs in resealable plastic bags.

Most recipes require your oregano to be dried. It can be air-dried in just a few days, by hanging it in a warm, dry area out of the sun. Oregano can also be dried in a dehydrator with a screen. The leaves are so small and dry so fast there is no need to dry this herb using the oven or microwave. Store your dry herb in airtight containers.

Culinary Uses

Oregano is traditionally used in the cultures descended from the Mediterranean world: Italian, Greek, Brazilian, Mexican, Spanish, and Cuban cuisines all use the herb extensively. It enhances egg and cheese dishes, goes well in yeast breads, vegetables, beef, pork poultry, game, tomato sauce, stuffing, and shellfish.

Italian Frittata

This is one egg dish that's not just for breakfast anymore.

> 3 tablespoons olive oil
> ¼ cup green onion, chopped
> ½ cup mushrooms, sliced
> ½ cup red and green peppers sliced
> 6 eggs
> ½ teaspoon parsley
> ⅓ teaspoon basil
> ½ teaspoon oregano
>   Salt and pepper to taste
> ¼ cup tomato sauce

Heat the olive oil in a skillet. Sauté onions, mushrooms, and peppers for about 5 minutes. Break eggs in a bowl and beat well. Pour over the vegetables and season with herbs, salt, and pepper. Slip spatula under omelet, allowing liquid egg to seep under and cook. Cook until the top is firm. Spread tomato sauce over top and turn in half. Serve immediately.

Oregano Cheese Bread

A great alternative to garlic bread, and it goes just as well with
Italian dishes.

    1   package yeast
    5¼ cups flour
    2½ cups shredded sharp
            cheddar cheese
    1¾ cups milk
    3   tablespoons oil
    2   tablespoons sugar
    2½ tablespoons minced oregano
            (4¼ tablespoons if fresh)
    1   teaspoon salt

In a large mixing bowl, combine yeast and 2 cups of the flour. In a pan, heat cheese, milk, oil, and sugar until warm. Do not boil. Add this to the flour/yeast mixture. Beat on low speed for about 30 seconds, then beat on high for 3 minutes. Stir in the rest of the flour, then combine with floured hands.

Knead in enough flour on a lightly floured surface to make a stiff dough. Knead for 8 to 9 minutes until the dough is elastic: when you pull it shouldn't break apart, and when you let it go it should spring back into shape. Shape dough into a ball and place in a greased bowl, turning once to grease all sides. Cover and let rise in a warm place until it doubles in size. This will take about 1 hour and 15 minutes.

Punch the dough down and divide in half. Cover and let set for 10 minutes. Shape into 2 loaves and place each in a buttered 8 x 4-inch loaf pan. Cover and let rise until double, about 45 minutes.

Bake at 350 degrees for 40 to 45 minutes. Cover with a piece of foil the last 10 or so minutes to prevent burning. Cool the loaves on racks.

Store-Bought Submarine Sandwiches

*That's what my kids call these because they taste like the sandwiches
we buy down the street at the submarine shop.*

½ cup vegetable oil
¼ cup vinegar
1 tablespoon oregano
1 onion sliced in thin rounds
Hoagie rolls
Swiss and American cheese
Ham
Salami, sliced tomatoes
Half a head of lettuce, chopped

Combine vegetable oil, vinegar, and oregano in a bowl. Cut open a hoagie
roll and layer on meats and cheeses. Layer tomato slices, onion, and lettuce.
Sprinkle on the oil mixture. Serve immediately or the bread will become
soggy.

Rice Pilaf Mix

*This is a wonderful mix to have on hand if you need a little side dish
with your meal.*

3 tablespoons garlic powder
3 tablespoons thyme
2 teaspoons allspice
2 teaspoons coriander
1 teaspoon black pepper
4 tablespoons oregano
¾ cup basil

Use 2 to 2½ tablespoons for each cup of rice. Prepare rice according to package directions and add the mix to the water before boiling.

Oven Veggies

Take this to the next potluck you're invited to. It's sure to raise some eyebrows, and everyone will be asking you for the recipe.

- 4 tablespoons melted margarine
- 2 eggs
- 1 cup dry bread crumbs
- ½ cup Parmesan cheese (fresh, please!)
- ½ teaspoon paprika (Hungarian is the best)
- ¼ teaspoon garlic powder (not garlic salt)
- ¼ teaspoon celery seed
  Dash of salt
- ½ teaspoon basil
- 1 teaspoon oregano
- ½ cauliflower, broken into florets
- ½ head broccoli broken into florets
  Mushrooms, sliced
  Red peppers, sliced in strips
  Carrots, sliced into strips
- 1 onion, sliced thin

Preheat oven to 400 degrees. Beat together melted margarine and eggs in a bowl. Combine bread crumbs, cheese, seasonings, and herbs in a large pie plate. Dip your veggies into the egg mixture and roll in the crumbs. Place on a greased cookie sheet and chill for at least 20 minutes. Bake for 15 to 20 minutes.

Sicilian Steak

Try this Italian-style steak. It'll become your family's favorite.

- 1 (2- to 2½-pound) round steak
- ¼ cup flour
- ¼ teaspoon salt
- ⅛ teaspoon ground pepper
- 3 tablespoons olive oil
- 1 (1 pound) can crushed tomatoes
- ½ teaspoon oregano
- 1 tablespoon chopped parsley
- ⅛ teaspoon dry mustard
- 1 clove minced garlic
- ½ teaspoon rosemary

Cut round steak into serving pieces, then pound thin with a tenderizing hammer or other hard object (my favorite method is to cover the steak with wax paper and pound it with the 6-inch section of a two-by-four—works great!). In a deep pie pan, mix flour, salt, and pepper and dredge meat in this mixture. Brown meat with oil in a large skillet.

Pour off liquid, add tomatoes, oregano, mustard, parsley, garlic, and rosemary. Cover and simmer about 1 hour.

Italian Barbecue Chicken

Keep in mind that most Italians (at least the ones I know) tend to cook for an army of hungry mouths. This recipe really makes a good deal of chicken.

        2 cloves garlic, finely chopped
        1 cup chopped parsley
        1 bay leaf
        1 tablespoon dried oregano leaves
        3 (1-pound) cans crushed tomatoes
        2 teaspoons salt
        ½ teaspoon pepper
        ¾ cup grated Parmesan cheese (fresh)
        4 (2- to 2½-pound) broiler fryers,
               halved and skinned
        ½ cup vegetable oil

Combine garlic, parsley, bay, oregano, tomatoes, salt, and pepper in a medium saucepan. Bring to boil and reduce heat. Simmer for 20 minutes.

Stir in the cheese and keep warm. Brush all sides of the chicken with vegetable oil and place on the grill, flesh side up.

Grill for 15 to 20 minutes, basting several times with sauce. Turn and fill cavities with sauce. Grill 15 minutes longer, basting. Serve.

Pizza Sauce

This is the best pizza sauce, bar none.

1   tablespoon olive oil
¼   cup finely chopped onion
1   (1 pound 3 ounces) can whole tomatoes
1   (8 ounce) can tomato sauce
1   bay leaf
¼   teaspoon salt
1   teaspoon sugar
2   teaspoons oregano
¼   teaspoon pepper

Heat the oil in a 2-quart saucepan. Sauté onion until brown. Drain tomatoes, saving the liquid. Crush tomatoes with a fork.

Now combine sautéed onions, tomatoes, and liquid, and rest of ingredients in the saucepan. Bring to a boil. Reduce heat and simmer for about 30 minutes, stirring occasionally. Remove bay leaf from sauce and spread on pizza dough.

REMEDIES

Oregano is mainly a culinary herb, but it can be used in a few remedies. Poultices have traditionally been used for sore, aching muscles and scorpion bites. Oregano tea has been used for chronic cough and asthma.

Refer to chapter 1 for information about preparing oregano in infusions, etc., and please see the medical disclaimer in the introduction of this book.

Use common oregano for all remedies.

Swelling—Make a poultice from oregano leaves and leave it on until the swelling begins to lessen.

Arthritis—Take 2 tablespoons olive oil and add 1 tablespoon oregano leaves. Steep for 1 day. Strain and use as a massage oil for arthritis.

Nervous Headache—Take a strong infusion to relieve nervous headache.

Measles—An infusion will bring on perspiration and bring out measles.

Seasickness—Take an infusion of the flowers only to relieve seasickness.

Toothache—Put a few drops of oregano oil on the tooth to stop pain.

ORNAMENTAL USES

Flowers of oregano dry nicely and can be used in flower arrangements or as part of a culinary wreath.

OTHER USES

In the Middle Ages, furniture was scoured with oregano to imbue its aromatic juices in the wood.

Dye made from oregano will turn wool purple and linen a reddish brown.

Oregano used to be an ingredient in beer, lending the beverage flavor and also helping to preserve it.

11

PARSLEY,
MORE THAN JUST
A GARNISH

Parsley is a common plant in any garden. Most people use it only as a garnish, little realizing the magic contained within this little herb.

Traditionally associated with fertility, it has the odd characteristic of taking its own sweet time to germinate. Perhaps that's why people thought of pregnant mothers and babies when they came upon a patch of parsley.

There are three varieties, two of which can be found in most any garden.

129

TYPES OF PARSLEY

Curly Leaf Parsley—This variety has ruffled, bright green leaves and grows to about 4 to 5 inches. It is used mostly as a garnish but can be used for culinary purposes.

Flat Leaf or Italian Parsley—With toothed, darker green leaves, this variety of grows to about 48 inches high. It is the one most commonly used because it contains the most flavor and value, particularly when used in remedies.

Parsnip or Hamburg Parsley—The last kind of parsley is rarely seen, at least above ground. The plant resembles the plumage of a carrot, with its root more often seen sold as "celery root."

All of these varieties are very high in iron, and vitamins A and C.

HISTORY, MAGIC, AND FOLKLORE

Parsley originates in the Mediterranean region. The ancient Greeks used parsley in funeral rites by weaving it into wreaths and decorating tombs. This accounts for the Greek association of parsley with oblivion and death. Wreaths were also given to winning athletes of the Nemean games, perhaps because of the belief that Hercules chose parsley for his personal garland. A legend is reported in the writings of several Greek authors that parsley sprang from the blood of the young hero Archemorus as he was dying near the walls of Thebes.

Romans put parsley on their plates with food to protect it and themselves from contamination. Racehorses were given plenty of parsley in the days of the

Roman Empire: the herb was thought to provide the animals with extra stamina. There is probably something to this practice, when you consider all the vitamins and minerals contained in the little plant. In the Bible, Saint Peter calls it a sacred plant.

By the Middle Ages, though, parsley took on a negative attribute. It was believed that parsley would grow and thrive only if it was planted by a person whose soul was wicked. This is probably due to the poor rate of fertility

and length of time the seeds took for germination. The wickedness theme carries over in a legend claiming that parsley belongs to the devil: it is
supposed to journey to the devil seven times
before it grows, and sometimes it even forgets to
come back. This is definitely a reference to its long
sprouting time.

The emphasis on long germination time has
been turned in folklore into a symbol for fertility in
general: so, according to folklore, if a pregnant
woman plants parsley it is more likely to grow.
This tradition states that wherever it grows a
woman is mistress of her house. In some regions it is even thought that sowing parsley enables a woman to conceive.

In seventeenth-century England it was said that newborn girls were found
in parsley beds, sort of an herbal equivalent of the "stork bringing the baby"
story. The babies were "harvested with care" and wrapped in clean white blan-
kets. This tradition led people to decorate with parsley for baby blessing rites.

Moving parsley is said to be bad luck, probably because it transplants
poorly. It is also bad luck to give parsley away, or to be given it. If a stranger
plants it in your garden, this is equally unlucky.

In the Victorian language of flowers parsley means festivity. This is probably because of the time-worn practice of using it as a garnish on plates of
food when entertaining.

Magic users partake of parsley in purification baths, to protect the home
and self, and to balance the inner male and female. According to folklore, it's
best to pick parsley on a Friday during the waxing of the moon. Another story
says that parsley must not be cut when harvested, lest you "cut" yourself off
from the one you love; rather, the needed amount should be plucked from
the plant. When eaten, parsley promotes fertility and fidelity.

Death imagery lurks around this plant, and there are several warnings against planting under the wrong circumstances. One of these suggests that parsley seeds be planted only on Good Friday, by the light of a rising moon. To ignore this advice is to invite the angel of death to your home. This fear of inviting death is still held by the Pennsylvania Dutch, who will not plant parsley too close to their houses, since they believe it might cause a death in the family.

PROPAGATION AND CULTIVATION

Parsley is a biennial. This means the plant will be lush and useful for the first year, then will come back the second year but go to seed early. To avoid inconsistent harvests, parsley should be treated as an annual and planted every year.

Since it takes a full 6 weeks to germinate, plant four times as much seed as needed. You may plant seeds after the ground has thawed and can be worked, when the air temperature is about 50 degrees. Barely cover the seeds with soil and sprinkle hay over the top. It will seem like it takes forever for them to sprout, about from a little over a week to more than a month. To speed up germination, put the seeds on a sponge in a saucer and keep the sponge moist. Once they have sprouted, place them in the area you want your parsley to grow, barely covering with soil, then covering the area with hay. You can also soak your seed in water, freeze for two days, thaw, and plant as described above.

Situate your parsley in full sun to partial shade. It prefers cool weather and lots of moisture. After your seedlings sprout and become about an inch high, thin to 8 inches apart. When your seedlings have become full-fledged plants, give them a trim 2 times a month to promote more growth. When flower stalks appear, make sure to cut them back.

Fertilize with liquid fertilizer at least once a month. Parsley can take temperatures down to 40 degrees before it needs protection.

Parsley grows very well in containers. It will continue to be good for 6 to 9 months. After that, plant more seeds and begin again. If your containers are outdoors in the summer and you have a cold winter, bring them in when it becomes cold: your parsley will continue to thrive inside.

Mix your parsley seed with carrot seed and plant the two together. This will repel carrot flies by masking the odor of the carrot. You may be confused when the plants first emerge from the ground, since it's pretty hard to tell which plant is which in the early stages: be patient. You'll be able to tell them apart in just a little while. Also keep in mind that the carrots should sprout before the parsley.

Parsley is affected by crown rot and nematodes. It can also be harmed by a green caterpillar with black stripes. This caterpillar transforms itself into the black swallowtail butterfly, which is an endangered species. You may want to plant a crop in one end of your yard just for this insect; it's well worth it just to see this beautiful butterfly. This should be the only serious threat to your crop.

Parsley enhances the scent of roses when planted nearby. It also protects roses from the rose beetle and repels the green fly. Tomatoes and asparagus love to be planted near parsley because it gives extra vigor to all involved.

HARVEST

Parsley can be harvested at any time.

STORAGE

Parsley can be frozen and used in stews and soups, though it tends to be a little limp when thawed. You can crumble your parsley while it is frozen and use in any dish. The flavor of the frozen herb is superior to dried.

Parsley can be dried several ways. Place on a screen or on newspaper and air-dry in a warm place, out of sunlight. Spread out parsley on a cookie sheet and place it in a 100-degree oven leaving the door open slightly at the top. Watch your parsley when using this method so that it doesn't burn: you may have to stir it around a little. Microwave your parsley by placing it between paper towels and microwaving on high for 1-minute intervals until dry and crisp. Store in airtight glass containers.

CULINARY USES

Both curly and flat parsley can be used as a garnish, bearing in mind that the flavor of flat is preferred over curly. Use hamburg parsley like a parsnip, utilizing only the white root.

Parsley Butter

The flavor of parsley goes with anything. This butter can be spread on bread or melted over any vegetable.

>   ½ pound butter (not margarine)
>   3 tablespoons parsley
>   1 tablespoon lemon juice
>   1 teaspoon brown mustard

Combine and roll into a log on wax paper. Wrap in paper and place in airtight plastic bag. Cut and use on new potatoes and green beans.

Fines Herbes

You're more than likely to find a recipe that calls for fines herbes if you do any cooking. Here is how to make it.

>   4 tablespoons dried parsley
>   2 tablespoons dried chives
>   2 tablespoons dried chervil
>   1 tablespoon tarragon

Mix together and keep in a jar. When needed, place the prescribed amount in cheese cloth, tie off and toss into the stew, soup, or whatever else you may be making.

Parsley and Fish Chowder

Parsley gives this fish chowder a mild and well-rounded flavor.

2 tablespoons butter
1 onion, chopped fine
1½ pounds haddock, filleted
  and cut into small pieces
1 pound potatoes, peeled, cut in
  slices ¼-inch thick
Salt and pepper to taste
1¼ cups light cream
6 tablespoons chopped parsley

Heat butter in a soup pot. Add onion and sauté. Lay the ingredients in layers on top of the onion as follows:

Fish
Potatoes
Salt and pepper

Add enough hot water to come level with top of potatoes and bring to a boil. Cover and simmer for 1 hour. When potatoes are soft, heat the cream in another pan and add to the chowder. Stir gently and add parsley. Serve immediately.

Parsley Sandwich

You're guaranteed to raise a few eyebrows if you bring in a brown bag lunch with this sandwich.

8 slices whole-wheat bread with the crusts removed
Butter
Cream cheese
¼ cup chopped parsley
Pepper to taste

Spread 4 slices of the bread with butter, the other 4 slices with cream cheese. Strew parsley on the cheese and grind on pepper if desired. Cover with buttered slices and cut in quarters.

Parsley Soup

This soup has a rich and interesting flavor.

> ½ cup butter
> 1 large onion, sliced thin
> 2 large carrots, sliced thin
> 1 large potato, peeled and sliced thin
> 3¾ cups chicken stock, heated
>   Salt and pepper to taste
> ¾ cup dried parsley leaves

Heat butter in a soup pot and add onion and carrot. Sauté about 6 minutes, stirring constantly. Add potato and heat for 3 minutes. Add heated stock. Add salt and pepper and simmer covered for about 35 minutes. Let cool slightly. Purée mixture in the blender, a little bit at a time with the parsley, and reheat.

Parsley Dumplings

These little wonders can be added to soups or stews.

> ½ cup all-purpose flour
>   Pinch of salt
> 2 tablespoons butter
> 1 large egg
> 1 tablespoon chopped parsley

Sift flour into a bowl with salt. Cut in butter in small pieces. Beat egg with parsley in a small bowl. Stir this into flour mixture and beat until smooth. This can be done with a food processor or an electric mixer.

Drop by the teaspoonful into a pan of boiling salted water. Cover and boil gently for 5 minutes. Lift lid and turn dumpling over. Boil 5 more minutes.

Dumplings can also be cooked with stew by dropping them into the pot and boiling gently, 10 minutes covered, then 10 minutes uncovered.

Herbie Pie

This pie has a quiche-like quality and is very delicious.

      1½ cups parsley
       1 cup fresh spinach
     2–3 Lettuce leaves
       ½ cup watercress
          Salt to taste
       1 teaspoon salt
       1 tablespoon flour
       1 pint heavy cream
       2 eggs, beaten
       1 9-inch pie crust

Heat oven to 325 degrees. Blanch the greens (parsley, spinach, lettuce, and watercress) for 3 minutes. Drain and squeeze out all moisture. Chop and sprinkle with salt. Spread on the bottom of a deep-dish pie plate. Mix the 1 teaspoon salt and flour in a bowl. Add cream and stir. Add eggs and mix well. Pour over the greens in the pie plate. Place a rolled-out crust over these ingredients and flute edges.

Bake in the preheated oven for 35 minutes. Cool slightly before serving.

Fried Parsley

*This tasty garnish offers a little more variety than just sticking a
piece of parsley on the plate.*

       1 large bunch parsley
          Vegetable or olive oil

Wash sprigs in cold water and dry by patting with a soft dish cloth (not terry cloth) or a paper towel. Heat enough oil in a frying pan oil to cover the bottom and come up the sides about ¼ of an inch. Heat to 170 degrees. Drop in sprigs, a few at a time, and cook 3 minutes, turning once. They will turn bright emerald green. Lift out and drain on paper towels. Serve immediately.

Parsley Stuffing

Stuff your chicken with this and it will be better than Thanksgiving. Speaking of Thanksgiving, if you want to use this stuffing for your turkey, just double the recipe.

6 ounces shallots (don't use green onions: shallots have the right delicate taste)
Butter (enough to coat skillet)
3 cups soft white bread crumbs (make your own in the blender)
½ cup chopped parsley
Salt and pepper to taste

Peel shallots and chop fine. Melt butter in a skillet and fry until golden. Add bread crumbs and stir until well mixed. Remove from heat and stir in parsley. Add salt and pepper. Cool completely before stuffing a chicken or turkey as this will prevent food poisoning.

Always bear in mind that food poisoning is a danger whenever you stuff a bird. If you really want to be safe, add some chicken or turkey broth to the stuffing and bake it in a casserole dish instead of in the bird.

REMEDIES

Parsley is traditionally used to control urinary infections and stones. It is also used as a diuretic or to rid the body of excess water. Parsley has many beneficial minerals and vitamins, containing more vitamin C per volume than an orange. It also contains vitamin A, several of the B vitamins, calcium, and iron.

Refer to chapter 1 for information about preparing parsley, and please see the medical disclaimer in the introduction of this book. As with several of the herbs discussed in this book, do not use parsley if you are pregnant.

Use flat leaf parsley for all remedies.

Kidney Infection—Make an infusion of the leaves or a decoction of the seeds and take 2 to 3 times per day. Do this for only 2 days in a row.

—Chop 3 cups parsley and add to 4 cups milk. Heat this on stove but do not boil. Reduce liquid to half. Cool and strain. Take 2 tablespoons every 2 waking hours for 2 days. Stop one day and, if needed, take for 2 more days.

If you take these kidney remedies for more than the prescribed amount of days, you can strip your body of beneficial vitamins and minerals, causing an even bigger problem.

Kidney Stones—Make a strong infusion and add the juice of 1 real lemon and 1 tablespoon olive oil. Drink once daily for 1 week.

—Grind parsley to extract the juice and drink once daily for several days. You can add carrot juice to make it more palatable. Parsley juice dissolves the stones.

Water Retention—Make an infusion of the leaves or a decoction of the seeds and take 2 to 3 times per day for 2 days.

Hemorrhoids—Take an infusion 2 times a day for 2 days. If the hemorrhoids don't disappear, try another 2 days AFTER a 2-day rest.

Gout—An infusion encourages production of uric acid, which eliminates gout.

Milk Production—An infusion once daily for 3 days will increase milk production and tone the uterine muscles. Do not use if pregnant.

Boils—Place a handful of parsley in a cheesecloth. Place this in hot water and wring out. Apply to boil for about 15 minutes. Place in hot water again, wring out, and apply for another 15 minutes. This should bring the boil to a head.

Indigestion—To ease an upset stomach, take a strong infusion steeped until cold and reheated before being drunk.

Scratched Eyes—Make an infusion with calendula and use warm. This should soothe scratched eyes, or help if you have a foreign particle in your eye.

Insect Bites—Rub fresh crushed parsley on the bite; this should reduce swelling. If swelling doesn't go away, or if there are other symptoms, such as fever or discoloration of extremities, go to the emergency room immediately.

Cosmetic Uses

Parsley is good for many cosmetic uses, from beautifying hair to removing freckles.

For dandruff, combine 4 cups boiled water and 2 tablespoons parsley. Steep until cool, strain, and rinse your hair. Pour it over your head, catching the excess liquid in a basin, then repeat 20 times.

For severe cases of dandruff, combine 1 pint boiling water, ½ cup chopped parsley, and 2 cups apple cider vinegar. Massage into your scalp and keep on for 15 minutes. Rinse out with water and use the above hair rinse. Your dandruff should be just a memory in about a week, if you use this treatment daily.

Parsley juice removes browns spots on hands and face. Grind fresh parsley to extract the juice, or make it easier on yourself and buy it in a health food store. Pat on affected area at night before going to bed.

Parsley infusion will remove freckles and moles. Dab on before going to bed at night.

For clogged pores and acne, make a strong infusion and cool to room temperature. Strain and apply the liquid to face as a compress for about 15 minutes. Do this daily until your complexion clears.

Skin Ointment

*This recipe works wonders as an ointment for use on pimples,
acne, or sores.*

> 1 cup packed fresh parsley
> 1½ tablespoons wheat germ oil
>   (found in health food stores)
> ½ cup petroleum jelly

Mix in a pan and cook on low heat for 30 minutes. Strain through a cheese-cloth and store in a covered jar. Apply at bedtime.

ORNAMENTAL USES

Parsley is good as edging for the borders of flower gardens. Curly leaf works best for this purpose.

OTHER USES

Put fresh parsley in your dog's moist food, then add dry food on top. It will keep the pooch's breath clean and fresh.

To take care of your own bad breath, dip 2 sprigs in white vinegar and chew. Parsley has been used as the antidote for garlic breath for over 2,000 years.

Rub parsley on exposed skin to repel mosquitoes.

12
THYME, THE PURIFYING HEALER

There are many varieties of thyme, each with their own special flavor and scent. Thyme is well-known for its uses in cooking, but in the past it was just as commonly used for fumigating sickrooms. The herb was even used as a preventative agent when the Black Plague was ravaging seventeenth-century England.

Thyme is a small, multi-branched shrub. The leaves are oblong, about ¼ to ½ inch, with the edges rolling under. The underside of the leaves is hairy. Flowers are small and

143

trumpet-like, ranging from white to lilac to pink, and growing in clusters. It flowers in June and July.

Folknames for thyme include Garden Thyme or Common Thyme. Botanically speaking, there are two classifications for the varieties of thyme: upright (growing in an erect manner) and creeping (used for ground cover). Both types are edible, but the upright classification has a better flavor.

A selection of the herb's 400 varieties is listed below. "U" means it is an upright, while "C" means it is of the creeping classification.

TYPES OF THYME

Camphor (U)—Grows 6 to 12 inches with dark green leaves and camphor scent. This variety needs a mild, dry climate.

Lemon (U)—Grows 4 to 12 inches with dark green, glossy leaves and a strong lemon scent. This is often used in fish and chicken dishes.

Silver (U)—Grows up to 10 inches with white-edged, silver-gray leaves. It is good in hanging baskets and used most often as an ornamental.

Common (U)—Grows 6 to 15 inches, with oval, gray-green leaves and tiny white to lilac flowers. This is the variety most often used in cooking.

Caraway (C)—Grows 2 to 5 inches with shiny dark green leaves, lavender to rose flowers. It has a caraway scent. This is one thyme that is excellent for culinary and ornamental uses. It makes a great ground cover, filler for rock gardens, looks great in a hanging basket, and can be used in soups and with meats and vegetables.

Nutmeg (C)—Grows to 4 inches with short, fat stalks and pink flowers. It is a fast creeper and has a nutmeg or spicy scent.

Mother-of-Thyme (C)—Grows to 4 inches with dark green leaves and pink blooms. When used as ground cover it forms a thick dense mass and is good as filler between steppingstones.

Wooly (C)—Grows up to 2 inches and has small, silver-gray leaves and tiny rose pink flowers. Used in walkways or rock gardens.

Albus (C)—Grows up to 5 inches, with green leaves and white flowers. Works well between steppingstones and flagstone.

Coconut (C)—Grows up to 4 inches, with a coconut scent and crimson flowers. Use as ground cover.

Golden (C)—Grows up to 8 inches with yellow green leaves. Use as ornamental ground cover only.

HISTORY, MAGIC, AND FOLKLORE

"Thúmon," as the ancient Greeks called it, represented style and elegance: they used it as a purification herb, burning it in their temples to cleanse the atmosphere around the sacred precincts. This carried over to the Middle Ages, when thyme represented chivalry and knightly honor.

Folklore concerning thyme states that if a maiden wears thyme in her hair, she will become irresistible to men and is marked as available for marriage. Another legend declares that it is dangerous to carry a branch of thyme into the house of an sick, elderly man, for he will surely die once the thyme enters his presence. In the Victorian language of flowers, and in magic, thyme represents courage and strength.

Thyme tea is drunk by many people to enhance clairvoyance. Thyme can also be worn on the body for the same effect. A pillow stuffed with thyme will cure nightmares and enhance deep sleep.

A sprig worn to a funeral will protect the wearer from any negative energy. Since thyme was used to purify Greek temples, it can be used equally well to purify homes or specific areas. Give thyme incense to celebrate a new home: this will act as a house blessing and encourage health in its inhabitants. Thyme can also be used as a purifying bath to wash away the negativity of the past.

Thyme is said to bestow the ability to see fairies and their domain. Some say any variety of thyme will do the trick, others say only wild thyme can work this magic. Tea drunk, incense burned and inhaled, a sprig carried, or the herb placed on the eyelids while sleeping on a fairy hill can bring about communion with these magical creatures. It is also said that where wild thyme grows, a powerful earth energy center lies nearby.

PROPAGATION AND CULTIVATION

Thyme is a perennial, reappearing every spring. Care must be given, however, as the branches can become woody, thick, and unproductive after many years.

Sow seeds indoors in March or April. Use a plastic bottle bottom and plant about 20 seeds. Thyme needs 70 degree bottom heat to germinate and the seeds must be kept moist, so use the plastic tent or glass cover method described in chapter 1. Germination takes less than one week. Two weeks after germination, feed the seedlings a little fish emulsion or skim milk diluted with some water. Take the young plants outdoors after 4 weeks have passed, but keep them protected at night. Move into the garden 1 week later.

For best results, plant your thyme in full to partial sun in an alkaline soil. Thyme will grow anywhere, but it prefers a sweet soil. Plant near eggplant and potatoes to enhance the growth of both. Thyme repels cabbageworm and whitefly.

Divide and take cuttings any time from spring through midsummer. Layering also works well in propagation. To take a cutting, cut a 3-inch piece from new growth. Place in wet sand and keep moist for two weeks until roots appear and growth is observed. Transplant into individual pots and plant in the garden when the weather is warm enough.

Most varieties of thyme do well in containers. The creeping variety creeps over the edge of the pots and cascades down.

Thyme is susceptible to fungal diseases and spider mites. Protect your thyme in the winter by placing a mulch of hay or leaves around it.

HARVEST

Thyme can be cut any time it is growing, though it is best if harvested before the blossoms open around midsummer. A major harvest can be taken at the end of June by cutting the entire plant 2 inches about the ground. You will be able to get a second harvest early in August. Do not trim close to the ground after the middle of August or the plant won't survive the winter.

STORAGE

Dried thyme is the best for storing. Thyme can be dried by hanging in bunches. After it has dried, strip the leaves from the stems and store in airtight jars. The leaves can be stripped before drying and laid on a screen to dry. Thyme can also be frozen, but it becomes limp when thawed.

CULINARY USES

Thyme is good in French, Creole, and Cajun cuisines. That covers an incredible number of possible dishes. Try it in salads, with tomatoes, cucumbers, beans, potatoes, corn, peas, cheese, eggs, rice, and in breads and stuffings. Thyme goes well with most meats, including beef, veal, lamb, poultry, fish, and sausage, not to mention stews and soups. You can plan a complete dinner menu using this versatile herb, down to liquors and cheeses flavored with it.

The following are a select few thyme recipes.

Lemon Thyme Cranberry Relish

Try this at Thanksgiving instead of plain old cranberry sauce.

4 cups shredded red cabbage
1 cup shredded carrots
1 cup whole berry cranberry sauce
(not the jellied sauce)
2 tablespoons cider vinegar (for a
more delicate flavor use
rice or white vinegar; wine
vinegar can also be used)
1 small clove garlic, crushed
1 teaspoon fresh chopped basil
2 teaspoons fresh lemon thyme

Combine all ingredients, cover, chill, and serve cold.

Thyme-Flavored Beans

*This recipe is good when using fresh beans, but I have used frozen
without the blanching process and they've tasted pretty good.*

½ pound fresh green beans, snapped
or French cut
2 tablespoons butter
1 tablespoon fresh thyme
Salt and pepper to taste

Blanch beans in boiling water for 2 minutes and plunge into cold water. Drain
and dry with a paper towel, removing as much moisture as possible. Melt the
butter in a skillet and add the beans and thyme. Add salt and pepper to taste.
Cook until hot and serve immediately.

Marinated Olives

Spice up those dull, boring black olives with this recipe.

8 ounces oil-cured black olives
1 teaspoon olive oil
1 clove garlic, crushed
2 strips orange peel
¼ teaspoon grated lemon zest
1½ teaspoons fresh thyme, or
　　½ teaspoon dried
¼ teaspoon fennel seed
　　Pepper to taste

Mix all ingredients and marinate overnight or for at least 5 hours. Serve cold.

Thyme Fillets

A filling fish dish, this one won't leave you hungry an hour later: it's heavenly rich and tasty!

1 medium onion, chopped
1 large tomato, chopped
3 tablespoons butter
¼ teaspoon salt
¼ teaspoon pepper
½ teaspoon thyme
1 cup white wine
¾ cup heavy cream
1 pound fish fillets (whitefish or trout does nicely)

Sauté onion and tomato in butter. Add seasonings. Add wine and let come to a rolling boil. Remove from heat. Wait until boiling stops, add cream and stir in. Set aside.

Place fish in a buttered baking dish and cover with the sauce. Bake at 350 degrees for 20 minutes.

Herb Burger

Get a new taste out of the good old American hamburger.

 1 pound ground chuck (use chuck
        because regular hamburger
        tends to be too greasy and
        will fall apart on the grill, making
        a big mess)
 ½ teaspoon garlic powder
 1 teaspoon thyme
 1 tablespoon chives
 1 tablespoon parsley
 2 eggs, beaten

Mix all ingredients together. Form patties and grill until done.

Lemon Thyme Cookies

These have an interesting flavor, but don't be surprised if children won't choose these over chocolate chip cookies.

 2½ cups unbleached flour
 1 teaspoon cream of tartar
 ½ teaspoon salt
 1 cup butter
 1½ cups sugar
 2 eggs
 3 tablespoons dried lemon thyme

Sift flour, cream of tartar, and salt in a bowl. Combine butter with sugar in a mixer bowl. Add eggs and mix well. Work in flour mixture until well blended. Add thyme. Chill dough overnight. Roll into walnut-sized balls and bake on a greased cookie sheet 10 minutes at 350 degrees.

Herb Broth

This is a real crowd pleaser. You can double or triple this recipe and there still won't be any left when you go to clear the table.

> 1 can beef broth
> ½ of the broth can filled
>   with cranberry juice
> Fresh thyme to season
> Chopped fresh mint, chives, or parsley

Heat the broth, cranberry juice, and thyme. Serve garnished with one of the other herbs.

REMEDIES

As mentioned before, Europeans in the fifteenth through seventeenth centuries used thyme as a safeguard against the Black Plague. After that threat was over, the herb continued to be used for a variety of cures, including a soup of thyme meant to combat shyness, nervous disorders, and nightmares (not to mention hangovers). In World War I, thyme was used as an antiseptic.

Thyme was traditionally put into pillows and thought to relieve epilepsy and melancholy. It's most useful in treating complaints of the bronchial system, while it is more generally useful as a stimulant, antiseptic, and expectorant. It can be used to get rid of warts, to ease gout, stomach disorders, flatulence, headaches, coughs, and sore throats.

Refer to chapter 1 for information about preparing thyme in infusions, etc., and please see the medical disclaimer in the introduction of this book. There are many cases in which thyme should not be your first choice as a remedy, as you can see from the following list of warnings.

Do not use if pregnant.

Thyme may cause skin irritation if used externally.

Take internally in moderation, as the herb can overstimulate the thyroid gland, causing poisoning.

Do not take if using thyroid medication.

The essential oil, thymol, can cause dizziness in its pure form.

All these warnings may make you think twice about using thyme in a remedy. It really is quite safe when used in moderation and if you are not pregnant.

Use common thyme for all remedies.

Insect Bites and Bee Stings—Use thyme vinegar to ease swelling and pain. As always, if extreme swelling or difficulty in breathing occurs, call the paramedics or get to a hospital immediately.

Flatulence—Take an infusion for relief of intestinal gas.

Cough—An effective cough remedy can be made of thyme. Bring 1 pint of water to boil. Add 1½ ounces dried thyme. Cool to room temperature and strain. Add 1 cup honey. Shake to mix and keep refrigerated. Take 1 tablespoon several times a day for sore throat and cough.

Asthma—Boil 4 cups water and add 3 tablespoons thyme. Place on a heat-proof pad on a table or countertop. Cover the pot and your head with a towel and inhale the fumes for at least 10 minutes. The volatile oils will go directly to the lungs and open them up, making breathing easier.

Bronchitis—Use same inhalation method as for asthma. This also cuts through the buildup in the lungs, making it easy to cough up and expel infected mucus.

Colds—Use a strong infusion to induce sweating. This will bring down the fever.

Rheumatism—Add an infusion to the bath. Thyme can also be added to liniments and massage oil. It brings a warming sensation to the afflicted area.

Digestion—An infusion will soothe the digestive system, acting as an antispasmodic for the smooth muscle of the stomach.

Water Retention—Boil 1 cup water and add 1 teaspoon thyme. Steep 15 minutes, strain, and add honey for taste. Drink 1 cup per day for 1 week. This forces any excessive water retention out through the kidneys. Diabetics should be very careful when using this method.

Thrush—Add 1 tablespoon dried mint and 2 teaspoons dried thyme to 1 cup boiling water. Steep 30 minutes, covered. Cool and strain. Use as a mouthwash to ease thrush.

Impetigo—Pour 1 pint water into a pot. Add ½ cup rosemary and ½ cup thyme. Bring to a boil and simmer for 15 minutes. Strain and cool. Dip cotton balls in mixture and cleanse area several times a day. Make sure to throw away the cotton ball immediately and do not re-dip a used cotton ball, as the infected matter is very contagious. Make a new batch daily.

COSMETIC USES

An infusion can be used to rinse after shampooing. This will benefit all types of hair.

Thyme vinegar can be used as a suntan lotion. Be careful, though, as not all skin types can tolerate the sun at the same intensity. This treatment won't necessarily prevent a sunburn. Keep in mind that consistent, long exposure to the sun can lead to skin cancer, no matter what you protect yourself with.

For acne, combine 1¼ cups boiling water, 4 tablespoons fresh or 1 teaspoon dry thyme. Steep for 30 minutes, covered. Strain and keep for 1 week in the refrigerator. Use cold by dipping a cotton ball in the solution and applying to affected area. This is an astringent and it will clear acne. Use 2 times a week or everyday.

AROMATIC USES

The essential oil, thymol, is used in making colognes and after-shaves. Thyme infusions were traditionally sprayed in sick rooms to prevent epidemics and this will work to a certain extent today. Thyme added to a bath gives off a lovely scent and warms the body when overtaken by chills or cold weather. Six drops of the essential oil in the bath will bring on relaxation in about 15 minutes, rejuvenating the spirits.

ORNAMENTAL USES

Use as an edging plant. The creeping type is good in rock gardens, between stones, and in hanging baskets.

OTHER USES

Thyme can be burned outdoors to repel stinging insects. Thyme oil repels mosquitoes: just rub it on the skin (an infusion or thyme vinegar will work too, but the oil works much better).

Animals occasionally get hot spots, irritated, red areas on the skin that sometimes bleed and shed. To combat this malady, mix equal parts olive oil and oil of thyme. Apply to the hot spot with cotton balls. This will stop the itching and prevent infection. Use sparingly at first to ensure the animal does not have an allergy to the thyme.

To banish mildew, wash down the area with a strong thyme infusion.

13
HERBAL VINEGARS

As you might expect, the word vinegar means "sour wine" in French. When making herbal vinegars, always use a vinegar with 5 percent acidity (it should give this information on the label). You can use wine vinegar (not flavored but using actual wine), white vinegar (used only when color is important), apple cider vinegar, malt vinegar, or balsamic vinegar.

Vinegar has traditionally been used to enhance flavor in foods, but it is also known as a primitive antibiotic. An interesting example of this can be found in the Bible, where it is said that the Roman soldiers gave Jesus vinegar to drink, allegedly to cause further suffering. In fact, the Romans were offering what everyone at the time was drinking, since vinegar was commonly used to kill whatever bacteria were found in the local drinking water!

MAKING VINEGARS

Method 1—Wash your herbs by swishing in cold water. Be careful that you don't bruise the leaves. Remove damaged leaves. Pat dry with a paper towel and air dry. Any moisture on the leaves or in the jar can make your vinegar cloudy.

Pack the cleaned herb in a dry, sterilized quart jar. Press down with a wooden spoon (when vinegar is touched with anything metal it causes a chemical reaction, so only use a wooden spoon). Fill the jars with vinegar to within 1 inch of the top. Pack down and bruise the herb with your wooden spoon. Cover the opening of the jar with plastic wrap, then top it with the metal lid. Store in a dark place for 6 to 8 weeks.

Method 2—Use an enamel pan (remember, metal causes an unwanted chemical reaction) to heat your vinegar just below the boiling point. Don't let it boil or the flavor will not be right. Pour the vinegar over herbs that have been placed in a quart jar. The heat releases the oils faster but the acidity will be destroyed if it is too warm, thus changing the taste. Store in a dark place for 4 to 5 weeks.

After the prescribed time has elapsed for either method, strain your vinegar through paper coffee filters until you can strain the vinegar and the filter stays clean: you may have to use 4 or 5 filters before this is achieved. Pour your vinegar into sterilized bottles and add a sprig of the appropriate herb.

Containers for your vinegars can take many shapes. You can used recycled salad dressing bottles that have been cleaned and sterilized in boiling water, or use empty glass bottles. Jars are also a possibility. Check your area stores for bottles with corks in which to store your vinegars. Part of the pleasure of making your own vinegars is that you can choose aesthetically pleasing containers for storing and displaying.

Wax seals can be made for your bottles. This gives an extra seal and looks nice too. Place a 15½-ounce metal can (e.g., a tomato or kidney bean can) in a saucepan filled with water up to about 1 inch on the can. Melt one square of paraffin (be careful because paraffin ignites at a low temperature). Mix in ¼ cup of any combination ground cinnamon, cloves, nutmeg, and/or allspice. When the paraffin becomes liquid, remove from the heat and stir with a wood stick. Dip the capped end of the bottle in the wax, allowing it to dry a bit and dip again. Do this 3 times.

Take a 4- to 8-inch piece of ½-inch wide grosgrain ribbon and place mid-point of the ribbon over the center of the cap. Push it into the wax to secure. Hold the ribbon ends out of the wax, dip top end of the bottle in the wax, dry for about 30 seconds and repeat 3 times or until the ribbon doesn't show through the seal. If the wax becomes clear, add more spices.

Allow the cap to dry completely before touching the wax. If you don't, it will leave fingerprints. To open the bottle, score with a knife just below the cap and turn the lid. The wax and ribbon will remain on the cap.

Your vinegars will have an 18-month shelf life if kept in a cool dark place.

Culinary Uses

There are many delicious things you can do with your vinegars. Add basil vinegar to asparagus, tomato salad, and tomato soup, or add to Bloody Marys or tomato juice. Add chive vinegar to cooked broccoli and Brussels sprouts, and garlic vinegar to salads, cooked and raw spinach, or make sauerbraten. Mint vinegar is great when added to mayonnaise or whipped cream, fruit or bean salads; it even complements apple juice in an unexpectedly refreshing way. Add oregano vinegar to scrambled eggs and salads.

Basic Salad Dressing

This is a basic dressing. You can experiment with all of your culinary vinegars for different taste temptations.

> 1 cup olive oil
> ¾ cup herb vinegar
> 2 tablespoons dried herb

Combine ingredients in a closeable jar, shake, and pour on salads.

Pasta Sauce

Try this on spaghetti, rigatoni, corkscrews, bow ties, or any other type of pasta.

> 1 cup sour cream
> ¼ cup grated Parmesan cheese
> 2 tablespoons basil vinegar (try oregano, too)
> 2 tablespoons fresh chopped basil or
>   1 teaspoon dried (if you are
>   using oregano vinegar, use the herb
>   oregano)

Combine and toss with warm pasta.

Basil Honey Dressing

The sweetness of honey and the strong basil flavor of this dressing combine in a match made in gustatory heaven.

- 1 cup honey
- ⅓ cup basil vinegar
- 2 cloves garlic, crushed
- 2 teaspoons fresh chives
- 4 tablespoons fresh basil
- 2 tablespoons fresh parsley
- 1 tablespoon fresh oregano

Combine all ingredients and drizzle over sliced tomatoes or salads.

Broccoli Salad

The taste of this salad is truly transcendental.

- 1 bunch fresh broccoli
- ¼ teaspoon chopped chives
- ¼ teaspoon dried basil
- 6 ounces shredded cheddar cheese
- 6 strips cooked bacon, crumbled

Dressing
- 1 cup mayonnaise
- ½ cup sugar
- 2 tablespoons basil vinegar

Separate broccoli into flowerets and place half of them in a 9 x 9-inch casserole dish. Dust with herbs and top with half of the cheese and bacon. Repeat another layer.

Combine ingredients for the dressing. Pour over salad and marinate 20 minutes. Don't toss: serve as is.

Mushroom and Spinach Toss

Serve this instead of a green salad. It goes well with Italian dishes.

    2 tablespoons thyme vinegar
    ¾ teaspoon salt
    1 clove garlic, crushed
      Ground pepper to taste
    3 cups sliced fresh mushrooms
        (don't used canned)
   16 ounces fresh spinach, torn
    ¼ cup olive oil

Mix vinegar, salt, garlic, and pepper. Add mushrooms and toss. Let stand 15 minutes. Toss spinach and oil in a bowl until leaves look coated. Toss mushroom mixture with spinach and serve.

Marinated Veggies

This dish makes a splash at picnics.

    ¾ cup salad oil
    ½ cup flavored vinegar
        (give any of them try)
    2 tablespoons lemon juice
    3 tablespoons sweet onion (Vidalia
        onions are the best)
    1 teaspoon salt
    ½ teaspoon sugar
  4–5 cups fresh vegetables (raw carrots, zucchini,
        celery, cherry tomatoes,
        pea pods, broccoli, cauliflower,
        olives, and mushrooms)

Combine all ingredients (except veggies) in bowl. Pour marinade over the veggies, cover, and marinate 3 hours or overnight before serving.

Fancy Bean Salad
This isn't just any old bean salad.

  1 16-ounce can wax beans
  1 16-ounce can red kidney beans
  1 16-ounce can green beans
       (I prefer French cut)
  1 16-ounce can butter beans
  1 16-ounce can lima beans
  ½ cup bacon, cooked and crumbled
  1 large onion, diced
  ½ cup raw carrots, diced
  ½ cup green pepper, diced

Dressing
  1½ cups sugar
  1½ cups oregano vinegar
  ¾ cup vegetable oil
  1 tablespoon dried parsley flakes
  1 teaspoon dried oregano

Drain and rinse all beans. Combine in a bowl and add bacon, onion, carrot, and green pepper. Combine dressing ingredients and pour over the beans. Refrigerate 1 day before serving.

Chicken Thyme

This dish has an unusual flavor that will tickle your taste buds.

          4 chicken breasts
          3 tablespoons butter
          1 onion, chopped
          6 tablespoons thyme vinegar
      1½ cups chicken broth
             Salt and pepper to taste
             Dash of fresh thyme

Brown the breasts in a skillet with butter. Reduce heat and cover. When breasts are almost done, add the onion and turn the heat to low. Remove the chicken from the skillet when onion is almost see-through (which means it's done) and add the vinegar and broth. Turn heat to medium. Return chicken to the skillet and cook until liquid has evaporated and thickened.

German Potato Salad

This is much different than regular cold potato salad. My grandmother used to make this, and I have to admit that I didn't like it very much as a child. Now I wish she was still around to make it. This potato salad is served warm.

2 pounds potatoes, pared and sliced
     in thin rounds
  Salt to taste
⅓ cup bacon drippings
¼ cup thyme vinegar or garlic vinegar
1 small onion, minced
½ teaspoon salt
½ teaspoon paprika
6 slices of crisp cooked bacon, crumbled

Cook potatoes in a pot of salted water until tender. Drain. Cook bacon in a skillet. When crisp, remove from the pan to a paper towel to drain. Save the bacon drippings. In a small saucepan, heat bacon drippings, vinegar, onion, salt, and paprika. Place the cooked and drained potatoes in a large bowl, along with crumbled bacon and the dressing you just made in the small saucepan. Toss lightly, being careful not to break up the potatoes. Serve immediately.

The bacon is a must, which means you can't eat this salad every day—it probably won't hurt you once in awhile, unless you have a condition that could be worsened by it.

Sauerbraten

This is a German dish that will lend a gingery sweet flavor to beef.

1 cup red wine vinegar
½ cup garlic vinegar
½ cup Burgundy
2 onions, sliced
1 carrot, sliced
1 stalk celery, chopped
   A few sprigs of parsley
1 bay leaf
2 whole allspice berries
4 whole cloves
½ teaspoon salt
½ teaspoon pepper
4 pounds chuck pot roast
⅓ cup vegetable oil
6 tablespoons all-purpose flour
1 tablespoon sugar
½ cup crushed gingersnaps (yes, the secret
   ingredient is a cookie)

Combine the vinegars, Burgundy, onion, carrot, celery, parsley, bay leaf, allspice, cloves, salt and pepper in a large glass or ceramic bowl (not metal—remember how metal changes the chemical compounds of vinegar). Wipe the meat with a paper towel and place in the marinade. Refrigerate, covered, for about 3 days, turning several times to marinate evenly.

Remove meat from marinade and wipe dry. Heat the leftover marinade in a small saucepan.

Place a Dutch oven on the stove on low heat. Add vegetable oil when pot is hot. Dredge the meat in flour and place it in the pot. Brown very well on all sides. Pour in marinade, then simmer, covered, for 2½ to 3 hours, or until tender.

Strain liquid from the meat into a 4-cup glass measuring cup and skim the fat from the surface. Measure 3½ cups of the liquid. If there is extra, pour it out; if there is less than enough, add a little hot water. Heat in another saucepan.

Make a paste in a small bowl using ½ cup cold water, the rest of the flour, and the sugar. Add this into the liquid, bringing to a boil while stirring constantly. Add the gingersnaps and pour over the meat. Simmer, covered, for 20 minutes.

Remove meat to a platter and pour some of the gravy over the top. Serve in thick slices with more gravy.

OTHER USES

There are several cosmetic uses for your vinegars.

Make a vinegar bath from calendula, lemon balm, or mint vinegar. Steep leaves in 4 cups white or apple cider vinegar for 6 to 8 weeks. You can also add flower petals to your vinegars. For best results, strain the vinegar and fill half a bottle with it, then add an equal amount of spring water. Allow this to blend for a few days and use 1 cup in a bath. Straight vinegar is usually a little strong for a bath.

To make a facial rinse, place 2 cups of a chopped herb (calendula, chamomile, lemon balm, or mint) in 1 pint of vinegar. Set for 2 weeks, then strain. Place 2 tablespoons in a washbasin of water and rinse. Lemon balm is good for oily skin, chamomile is good for dry skin, and calendula works with acne-prone skin, while mint is a great astringent.

Make an after-shave by combining 2 cups thyme leaves with 1 pint cider vinegar. Set for 2 weeks and strain. This is a healing vinegar.

Thyme vinegar cures athletes foot and eases stings from insects. Thyme or basil vinegar will ease the itching and redness of hives. Add 1 ounce of the herb vinegar to 3 ounces cornstarch and dab on the hives. This is antiseptic and will heal them quickly.

Thyme vinegar repels mosquitoes and other insects.

Conclusion

Now you've seen many of the amazing things you can do with herbs. The longer you work with these green wonders, the more you will gain an appreciation of all that is around you, and you'll probably see things you never believed you would see. Who knows, you might even come in contact with the devas and fairies said to live within a garden's greenery.

In any case, as you continue your journey into the world of herbs, you will understand that all life on this earth is designed to work in harmony. The herbs and other plants of the earth nourish and heal our bodies. They enhance our lives and make our surroundings more beautiful. We humans, in turn, must make sure that the plants are cultivated and carry on for each succeeding generation. Planting seeds and young plants in our Mother Earth, watching them grow under caring attention, then harvesting the fruits of our labor and knowing how to use that harvest in many different ways is very satisfying, sublime experience.

It's time now for you to choose your herbs and get ready to plant. The subjects covered in this book serve only as a first step: once you have begun your journey into the magic world of herbs, there is no end to the creative powers you will come to recognize in yourself, your gardens, and in the earth. Enjoy!

GLOSSARY

Note: Some of the terms listed here can be used both as descriptors and as objects—e.g., "anesthetic," "diuretic," "aromatic."

Alum—A mordant used in dyeing.

Anesthetic—Causes the loss of feeling in a part of the body.

Annual—A type of plant that cannot withstand cold and will only live during one season.

Antibiotic—A substance that eliminates infection, kills germs.

Anti-inflammatory—Eases the pain of an inflammation.

Antiseptic—Prevents infection.

Antispasmodic—Substance that can cause muscles to relax.

Aromatic—Relating to scent.

Astringent—Cleanses or takes away oils from the skin.

Biennial—A plant which is fruitful in its first year and will return in the second season, but goes to seed early.

Blanch—To place a vegetable or other plant in boiling water, cover, and cook for a short time. The veggie should come out crisp, not mushy.

Bruise—To handle an herb so that it will emit its oils.

Combine—To mix all ingredients.

Cream—To beat until smooth and creamy.

Culinary—To cook.

Decoction—Root, bark, seeds, or stems of an herb are boiled in water and strained.

Dissolve—To make liquid with a dry substance going into the solution.

Diuretic—To increase the flow of urine thus eliminating waste products and toxins.

Division—Propagation method in which established plant is divided into two or more plants.

Dredge—To coat food with a dry ingredient, usually flour.

169

Elixir—Infusion of herb, alcohol, and a sugar such as honey.

Essential Oils—Scented plant oils used in herbal preparations.

Filtered Sun—Sunlight will be filtered through a shade of sheer curtain.

Flake—To break or pull apart food.

Flats—Planting containers.

Flatulence—Excessive intestinal gas.

Fold—To combine two ingredients gently using an under and over motion.

Germinate—Time it takes for a seed to sprout.

Harden Off—A gradual exposure to the elements.

Indirect Sun—Not directly in sunlight or in front of a window.

Inflammation—A reaction to injury or infection. Symptoms include swelling, redness, heat.

Infusion—Herb is steeped in water that has been boiled (tea).

Knead—To press dough with the heels of the hands so that the dough becomes stretched and elastic.

Laxative—Increases bowel movement.

Layering—Propagation method in which a branch of the established plant is pinned to the ground so that it grows roots, after which it is cut and transplanted.

Macerate—Soaked to be softened and dissolved.

Marinate—To soak in an acid to act as a tenderizer. Example: meat soaked in vinegar.

Mordant—Substance that causes a chemical reaction resulting in a certain color of dye.

Perennial—A type of plant that will appear to die when cold weather arrives, but will return the next season.

Planting Medium—Substance in which to plant seeds or new plants.

Potpourri—A mixture of dry herbs, spices, etc., that makes a pleasant scent.

Poultice—Bruised fresh herbs applied hot and covered in a hot cloth to relieve sprains bruises, etc.

Propagation—Method in which new plants are created.

Purée—To blend either fruits or vegetables until they are pulpy.

Reduce—To boil a liquid until the amount becomes smaller and more concentrated.

Root Cutting—Propagation method in which a root is taken from an established plant and is placed in planting medium to root.

Sauté—Gently fry until golden and tender.

Sprig—A branch of leafy stem from a plant or herb.

Steep—To extract oils and essence by soaking in water.

Stem Cuttings—Propagation method in which a stem is cut from the established plant and placed in planting medium to root.

Sterile Hybrid—A plant that does not produce seed. It must be propagated by other methods.

Sterilize—To heat in boiling water for 20 minutes in order to destroy germs.

Strewing Herb—Herb used in the Middle Ages. It was thrown about the floor in houses to produce a pleasant odor (and mask unpleasant ones).

Tincture—Made from an herb solution concentrate and alcohol.

Tisane—Infusion made from water and herb flowers.

Tonic—Invigorates organs or entire organism.

Toxic—Poisonous

Transplant—To move a plant from one area to another.

True Leaves—Second set of leaves a plant will produce.

Vermiculite—A planting substance, white in appearance, that holds water and makes the planting medium lighter and easier for the new plants to grow.

Volatile Oils—The oils from the plant that release vapors.

BIBLIOGRAPHY

Here is a list of my favorite books on herbs. They will give you even more information.

Magic & Medicine of Plants. Pleasantville: Reader's Digest Books, 1982.

Rodale's Illustrated Encyclopedia of Herbs. Emmanus: Rodale Press, 1987.

Castleman, Michael. *The Healing Herbs.* Emmanus: Rodale Press, 1991.

Cunningham, Scott. *Cunningham's Encyclopedia of Magical Herbs.* St. Paul: Llewellyn Publications, 1998.

——————. *Magical Herbalism.* St. Paul: Llewellyn Publications, 1997.

Dunwich, Gerina. *Wicca Garden.* Secaucus: Citadel Press, 1998.

Galenorn, Yasmine. *Embracing the Moon.* St. Paul: Llewellyn Publications, 1998.

Grieve, Mrs. M. *A Modern Herbal.* London: Dorset Press, 1994.

Hopman, Ellen Evert. *A Druid's Herbal.* Rochester: Destiny Books, 1995.

Hutchens, Alma R. *Indian Herbology of North America.* Boston: Shambhala Publications, 1973.

Leyel, Mrs. C. F. *Herbal Delights.* New York: Gramercy Publishing Company, 1986.

Maybe, Richard (ed). *The New Age Herbalist.* New York: Collier Books, 1988.

McIntyre, Anne. *Herbs for Common Ailments.* New York: Simon & Schuster (Gaia), 1992.

Newdick, Jane. *At Home with Herbs.* Pownal: Storey Communications, 1994.

Rose, Jeanie. *Jeanie Rose's Modern Herbal.* New York: Perigee Books, 1987.

Riotte, Louise. *Companion Planting for Successful Gardening.* Charlotte: Garden Way Publishing, 1976.

Shaudys, Phyllis V. *Herbal Treasures*. Pownal: Storey Communications, 1994.

——————. *The Pleasure of Herbs*. Pownal: Storey Communications, 1986.

Shelton, Ferne. *Pioneer Beauty Secrets*. High Point: Hutcraft, 1970.

Simmons, Adelma Grenier. *Herb Gardening in 5 Seasons*. New York: D. Van Nostrand Company, 1964.

Wilen, Joan and Lydia Wilen. *Chicken Soup and Other Folk Remedies*. New York: Fawcett Columbine, 1984.

Williams, Jude C., M.H. *Jude's Herbal Home Remedies*. St. Paul: Llewellyn Publications, 1992.

INDEX

RECIPES

REACH FOR THE MOON

Llewellyn publishes hundreds of books on your favorite subjects! To get these exciting books, including the ones on the following pages, check your local bookstore or order them directly from Llewellyn.

ORDER BY PHONE

- Call toll-free within the U.S. and Canada, 1-800-THE MOON
- In Minnesota, call (651) 291-1970
- We accept VISA, MasterCard, and American Express

ORDER BY MAIL

- Send the full price of your order (MN residents add 7% sales tax) in U.S. funds, plus postage & handling to:

  Llewellyn Worldwide
  P.O. Box 64383, Dept. K430-8
  St. Paul, MN 55164–0383, U.S.A.

POSTAGE & HANDLING

(For the U.S., Canada, and Mexico)

- $4.00 for orders $15.00 and under
- $5.00 for orders over $15.00
- No charge for orders over $100.00

We ship UPS in the continental United States. We ship standard mail to P.O. boxes. Orders shipped to Alaska, Hawaii, The Virgin Islands, and Puerto Rico are sent first-class mail. Orders shipped to Canada and Mexico are sent surface mail.

International orders: Airmail—add freight equal to price of each book to the total price of order, plus $5.00 for each non-book item (audio tapes, etc.).

Surface mail—Add $1.00 per item.

Allow 2 weeks for delivery on all orders.
Postage and handling rates subject to change.

DISCOUNTS

We offer a 20% discount to group leaders or agents. You must order a minimum of 5 copies of the same book to get our special quantity price.

FREE CATALOG

Get a free copy of our color catalog, New Worlds of Mind and Spirit. Subscribe for just $10.00 in the United States and Canada ($30.00 overseas, airmail). Many bookstores carry New Worlds—ask for it!

Visit our website at www.llewellyn.com for more information.

Herbal Gold: Healing Alternatives
Madonna Sophia Compton

Fact is, there are more degenerative diseases today than ever before: arthritis, heart disease, allergies, immune system deficiencies, chronic fatigue syndrome, and others. More and more, people are finding relief in herbs and other natural remedies. Now, you can find the most important herbs for your health in *Herbal Gold*, including new herbs such as the famous Cat's Claw from the Peruvian rain forest and Pycnogenol (pine bark). Discover the newest research on "adaptogens," wonder herbs with multiple actions that are 20-50 times stronger than vitamin C and other known antioxidants—and which may hold answers in the future for treatment of AIDS and cancer. Learn how to protect yourself and your family with specific phyto-nutrients, herbal combinations, a millennium herbal first-aid kit, and simple recipes and suggestions anyone can follow.

1-56718-172-4
6 x 9, 360 pp., softcover $12.95

Cunningham's Encyclopedia of Magical Herbs

Scott Cunningham

This is the most comprehensive source of herbal data for magical uses ever printed! Almost every one of the over 400 herbs are illustrated, making this a great source for herb identification. For each herb you will also find: magical properties, planetary rulerships, genders, associated deities, folk and Latin names and much more. To make this book even easier to use, it contains a folk name cross reference, and all of the herbs are fully indexed. There is also a large annotated bibliography, and a list of mail order suppliers so you can find the books and herbs you need. Like all of Cunningham's books, this one does not require you to use complicated rituals or expensive magical paraphernalia. Instead, it shares with you the intrinsic powers of the herbs. Thus, you will be able to discover which herbs, by their very nature, can be used for luck, love, success, money, divination, astral projection, safety, psychic self-defense and much more. Besides being interesting and educational it is also fun, and fully illustrated with unusual woodcuts from old herbals. This book has rapidly become the classic in its field. It enhances books such as *777* and is a must for all Wiccans.

0-87542-122-9
6 x 9, 336 pp., illus., softcover $14.95

Mother Nature's Herbal

Judy Griffin, Ph.D

A Zuñi American Indian swallows the juice of goldenrod flowers to ease his sore throat. An East Indian housewife uses the hot spices of curry to destroy parasites. An early American settler rubs fresh strawberry juice on her teeth to remove tartar. People throughout the centuries have enjoyed a special relationship with Nature and her many gifts. Now, with *Mother Nature's Herbal*, you can discover how to use a planet full of medicinal and culinary herbs through more than 200 recipes and tonics. Explore the cuisine, beauty secrets and folk remedies of China, the Mediterranean, South America, India, Africa and North America. The book will also teach you the specific uses of flower essences, chakra balancing, aromatherapy, essential oils, companion planting, organic gardening and theme garden designs.

1-56718-340-9
7 x 10, 448 pp., 16-page color insert, softcover $19.95